TURKEY

an amazingly short history

by
BOB FOWKE

Travelbrief Publications

Published in 2006 by Travelbrief Publications

0-9548351-2-3

10 9 8 7 6 5 4 3 2 1

Travelbrief Publications
7 Brougham Square, Shrewsbury SY3 7PE

Printed and bound by Cambrian Printers, Aberystwyth, UK

CONTENTS

MEHMET THE CONQUEROR
THE TURKS TAKE OVER — Page 5

A KILIM TOO FAR
THE VERY BEGINNING — Page 8

GREEKS AND ROMANS
HELLENISM — Page15

THE JEWEL OF THE WORLD
THE BYZANTINES — Page 29

WILD HORSEMEN
THE TURKS — Page 40

SULEIMAN THE MAGNIFICENT
AND THE SULTANATE OF WOMEN — Page 50

THE SOT AND OTHER BLOTS
THE SLIPPERY SLOPE — Page 58

HE WORE A GIANT SPOON
COOKING POTS AND A NASTY SPAT — Page 66

TOO MUCH SEX
OR NOT ENOUGH? — Page 79

WAR!

THE LAST OF THE SULTANS   Page 91

ALL CHANGE

ENTER THE HERO   Page 101

POSTSCRIPT

                                           Page 107

BYZANTINE EMPERORS   Page 110
SELJUK SULTANS   Page 114
OTTOMAN SULTANS   Page 115
IMPORTANT DATES   Page 117
INDEX   Page 122

INTRODUCTION

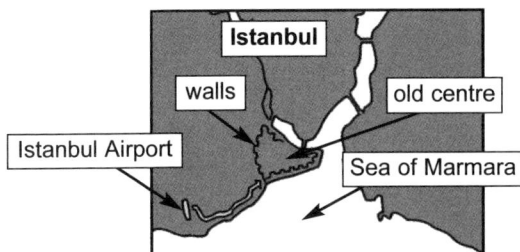

Along the coastal road from Istanbul airport, the trip into old Istanbul takes about twenty minutes. On the land side, housing developments crowd inward, interspersed with factories and stores and all the clutter of a modern great city. On the shore side there's sand and sea. The road skirts a wide bay with a fun fair and packed restaurants along the shore and, beyond the funfair, the wide waters of the Sea of Marmara seem to stretch out to infinity, only interrupted by the translucent humps of the Princes' Islands, far out and shimmering in the blue. On those islands, rebel princes and deposed emperors were first blinded and then imprisoned as a humane alternative to death, many centuries ago before the Turks arrived.

After the funfair there's another bay and a harbour where rusty container ships sleep beneath the skeletons of their derricks. Their names speak of middle earth: Russian, Georgian, Bulgarian, Turkish and Greek. The city centre is closer now and the pace of the traffic picks up. And now on the shore side, as the road rounds the corner into yet another bay - something extraordinary comes into view. A vast, ancient, fortified wall strides across the hills and plunges down to the sea. At the point where road and wall intersect, the road passes through a huge fortified

5

gate, recently reconstructed, the Golden Gate, and then the wall turns left to follow the road so that you're riding between sea and wall. The wall is immense, crumbling, ancient. In places it shrinks to nothing, in others houses are built into its very structure and trees grow from the towers. A train-line joins it and bridges a gap. On and on it goes. There's nothing like it outside of China.

That was how I first entered Turkey. In a taxi with the windows open so that I could smell the smells of the city. It was love at first sight. No other city on earth commands such a location. The road to Istanbul leaves you in no doubt that you are entering an extraordinary country.

However you first arrive, Turkey demands respect. The hills are big, the roads are long and the air blows in from the vastness of Asia. What I didn't anticipate on my first visit and what comes as a pleasant surprise to many visitors was the people. National labels and suchlike generalisations are of course slippery things and it's absurd to talk about a 'people' when real people are so complex, but it's a true nevertheless that the vast majority of Turks are dignified, good-humoured, polite and friendly. They are the very diverse product of an immensely long history, a mixture of all those who once inhabited this fabulous land and of their Turkish ancestors who rode in from the steppes of Asia, and they seem to have picked up most of the best characteristics of all of them.

This is a short history of Turkey, or rather, a history of the land which Turkey now occupies. No one culture can claim continuous ownership. Turks followed Greeks who followed Phrygians who followed Hittites, who wrested control from yet earlier centres of power. From this huge panorama peopled with giants such as Alexander the

Great, Cleopatra and Suleiman the Magnificent I have chosen those best fitted to illustrate their times, but I've had to leave out countless others who were equally or more colourful. I hope that they will forgive me and that you will too.

Bob Fowke
April 2006

WALLED OUT
THE TURKS TAKE OVER

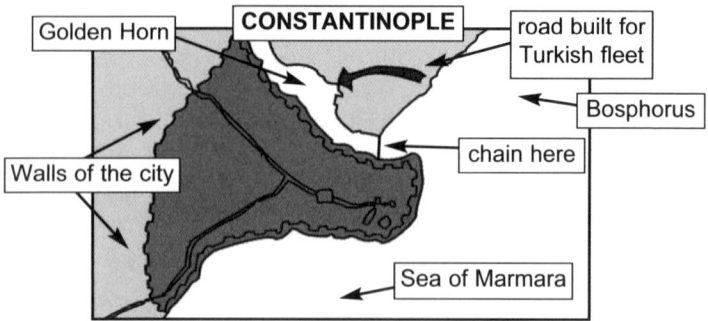

The Conqueror

On 22 April 1453, Christian defenders manning the mighty walls of Constantinople (Istanbul) woke to an extraordinary sight. On the far side of the waters of the Golden Horn, a fleet of ships was descending a hill over dry land. The leading ship was carried on massive wheels and was dragged by teams of oxen while its oars moved through the empty air to the beat of drums and the wail of flutes. Another seventy ships on wheels or rollers followed. Blocked from entering the waters of the Golden Horn by an immense chain slung across its entrance, the Turkish fleet had found an alternative route.

They could now attack Constantinople from several sides at once.

For six weeks, a tiny force of less than five thousand Christian, Greek defenders, led by their Emperor Constantine XI (1448-53), including monks and a handful of Italian fighters, had held off a huge Turkish army of more than 300,000 men led by their young, ambitious Sultan, Mehmet II.

The odds were hugely in favour of the Turks, but several of the Turkish commanders had been against Mehmet's plans for the siege. This was because the Greeks had one enormously powerful ally - the walls of Constantinople itself. For more than a thousand years, these walls had withstood twenty-nine attempts to take the city: by Arabs, Persians, Bulgars, savage Avars and Russ and many others. One by one these enemies had washed against the walls and then retired to lick their wounds. Only once, in 1204, had the walls been breached, by fellow Christians - by the Crusaders. The walls girdled the city in a massive collar of stone over twenty kilometres in circumference. On the landward side, there were actually two walls with a sixty foot ditch or killing ground between them. The walls rose to 40 feet on the inner wall and the towers to 60 feet, cleverly spaced so that those on the inner wall covered the gaps between those on the outer wall.

But now the Turks had gunpowder, quite a recent bit of technology, and an array of cannon to help them. One of the cannon was a twenty-eight-foot monster which could fire cannon balls weighing over six hundred kilograms (although, admittedly, it was so cumbersome that it could only be fired seven times a day).

Every night for six weeks the defenders, most of the active citizens of the city including women and children, had repaired the damage of the day. They patched with planks and sacks of earth. They hung bales of wool over the walls and covered them in leather to muffle the impact of the next day's cannon balls. One night, frustrated by the lack of progress, the Turks had attacked in force so as to hinder the repairs. After four hours of savage fighting the Turks had been driven off - and the Christians hadn't lost a single soldier. Greek armour was superb.

But now the Golden Horn was in Turkish hands and the Turks were confident of victory. They worked night and day to prepare for a final assault.

Sometime after midnight on 29 May, three columns, fifty thousand men in each, launched themselves from siege towers and ladders against the thin line of defenders. Within the city, church bells rang the alarm. Even nuns came running to pass stones and other ammunition to the soldiers - but all in vain. The overwhelming Turkish superiority in numbers at last began to tell. A breach was made in the outer wall and at the same time Turkish soldiers forced their way through a small doorway left loose after a sally by defenders. The Turks gained the inner wall. Emperor Constantine made one last, desperate attempt to rally his troops. Finally, after savage fighting and seeing that the end was near, he flung off his imperial markings and with a close companion plunged into the ocean of Turks, sword in hand. He was never seen again.

The following morning, Sultan Mehmet the Conqueror entered the city of Constantinople for the first time. After years of Turkish pressure, it was a shockingly desolate place. Large areas were completely uninhabited. As an emergency measure, he ordered a halt to the customary three days of looting allowed to the soldiers of Islam after a city had fallen. Then he rode to Haghia Sophia, the 'Church of Holy Wisdom', the central shrine of the City and of the Greek Byzantine Empire.

Even Mehmet must have felt a sense of awe on seeing this huge church for the first time. It was (and still is) an incredible sight, roofed by a vast dome which seemed to float on air, the largest building in the world then and for nearly a thousand years in total. And a beautiful sight too

- or it would have been if the floor hadn't been piled high with mounds of dead Greeks, massacred before Mehmet could call a halt.

Super power status

That moment in 1453 when Mehmet the Conqueror entered Haghia Sophia in the captured city of Constantinople was the key moment of Turkish history. Constantinople was the last toehold of Christian Europe in the land which would become modern Turkey and it was the last bastion of the once-mighty Byzantine Empire which had ruled that part of the world for many centuries. From that moment, the Turkish Empire became a super power.

It hadn't happened overnight. Over the previous centuries, Turkish power had spread slowly across what was then called Asia Minor and from there into Thrace, the south-east corner of Europe. Now, with Constantinople in his hands, the Turkish sultan controlled a huge chunk of the globe stretching uninterrupted from the borders of Persia (modern Iran) to the Greek heartlands. Within a further seventy-six years this Turkish giant had absorbed all of the Balkans and was hammering on the gates of Vienna.

Turkish History

1923	Republic proclaimed, capital moved to Ankara
1908	Young Turks seize power, national elections
1683	Second Siege of Vienna
1529	First Siege of Vienna
1520-66	Reign of Suleiman the Magnificent
1453	Turks capture Constantinople
1320s	Osman, first leader of the Ottomans establishes his power base.
1071-1243	Seljuk Empire
330-1453	Byzantine Empire
150 BC - AD 330	Roman dominated period
323 - 130 BC	Hellenistic period
334 - 323 BC	Campaigns of Alexander the Great
c.1450-1180 BC	Hittite Empire
c.8500-7500	Çatal Höyük, second oldest town in the world after Jericho

A rhino

Turkey looks a bit like a rhino's head. It straddles Europe and Asia. The European part is called Thrace, the Asian part, the rhinoceros, is called Anatolia.

At one time the word 'Asia' referred only to an area south of the ancient city of Troy. The word 'Asia' gradually came to mean all of what is now Anatolia and then went on to include all of the world's largest continent. To clarify matters, in the Roman period what is now Anatolia was known as 'Asia Minor'.

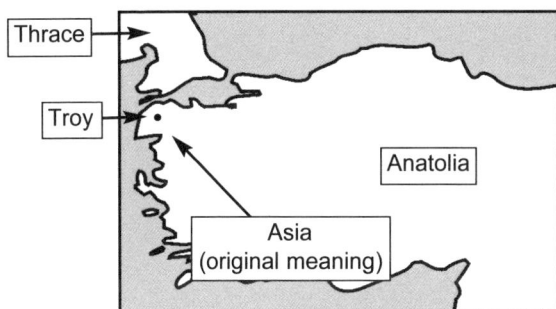

Anatolia itself, *anadolu* in Turkish, comes from Greek for 'sunrise' (*anatole*) and thus for 'the east' because the sun rises in the east.

Anatolia is shielded by mountains. To the south and east are the Taurus mountains. To the north along the Black Sea are the Pontic Mountains. In the east the two mountain systems collide in a remote region of high and craggy peaks, the highest being Agri Dag, the Cloven One - Mount Ararat as it's called in the Bible - where Noah's ark came to rest.

The centre of Anatolia is a high plateau where the water tends to drain inwards to the centre instead of outwards to the sea. It gathers in a number of lakes which are as salty as the Dead Sea. The biggest of them is Lake Van.

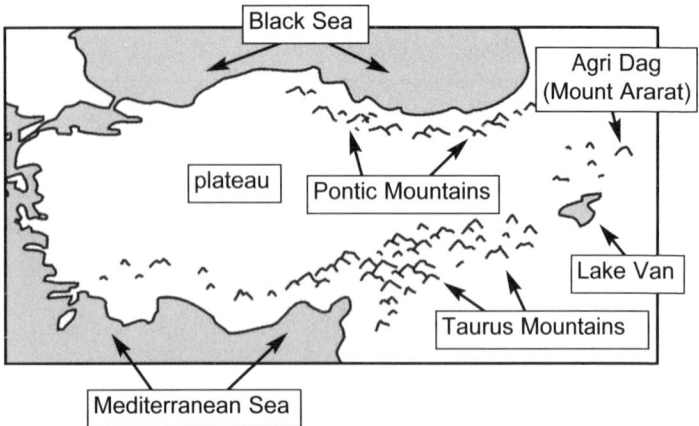

Black Sea

Agri Dag (Mount Ararat)

plateau

Pontic Mountains

Lake Van

Taurus Mountains

Mediterranean Sea

Talking Turkey

Turkey is a country but it's also the name of a bird. This is due to a misunderstanding. The 'Turkey-cock', as the species was once called, was a native of Mexico, but turkeys were first supplied to England via North Africa. This was because the first birds to be taken from Mexico were imported into North Africa by Spanish traders. And from North Africa, English merchants, known as 'Turkey Merchants' due to their trading links with the Muslim world, supplied the birds to England.

A KILIM TOO FAR

THE VERY BEGINNING

In Brief - from Alexander to Constantine

Before 7,500 BC   Çatal Höyük
c.1,750-1,180 BC   Hittite Kingdom then Empire
c.1,180-750 BC   Invasions and small kingdoms
c.750-600 BC   Phrygian supremacy
690-546 BC   Lydian golden age

Deep time

Until recently, no one had any idea how incredibly ancient the history of Turkey/Anatolia really is. Now we know better. Sixty kilometres to the south of Konya is the site of the second oldest city ever discovered (the oldest is Jericho in Palestine). Çatal Höyük was first inhabited *before* 7,500 BC. That's more than four thousand years before the Egyptian pyramids were built and three-and-a-half thousand years before the first stones were laid at Stonehenge. It was only discovered in 1961, by British archeologist James Mellart.

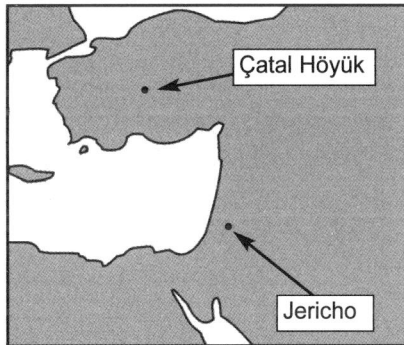

The people who lived in Çatal Höyük were tall by ancient standards, five foot ten on average for men and five foot two for women. We know this because they buried their dead inside their houses, underneath their beds, the men in one place the women and children in another. Only the

15

bones were buried. Paintings of vultures on the walls suggest that the corpses were first left outside to be picked clean by vultures, a practice followed by the Parsees to this day.

Çatal Höyük had no roads and the houses had no front doors. They butted up against each other and access must have been through the roofs. There's a map painted on an internal wall of one of the houses, the earliest map in existence, which shows this. It's clearly identifiable as a painting of Çatal Höyük by a volcano in the background.

Remains of some of the earliest woven fabrics ever discovered have been found in the floors of Çatal Höyük. There are also designs painted on the walls of some of the houses. James Mellart claimed that these designs were the ancestors of the patterns of the kilims still woven in that part of Anatolia today. If Mellart is right, then this adds up to quite an extraordinary span of cultural continuity, but most experts think that Mellart let his enthusiasm take him a kilim too far.

If you're visiting Konya

Çatal HöKük is less than an hour's drive from Konya. The excavations are unimpressive compared to great sites like Ephesus, but, of course, this site is far, far older. There's a small museum and, near the main entrance, a reconstruction of one of the mud houses.

Parcel in the post

There's a long gap between Çatal Höyük and the civilisation of the ancient Hittites, the first major culture of Anatolia, which got under way around 1750 BC. Nothing much was known about the Hittites until the early twentieth century.

The Hittite capital, which lies to the north of Çatal Höyük, was discovered in 1905 by Professor Hugo Winckler from Berlin, an expert on cuneiform, the writing system of the ancient Middle East. In 1904 he received a cuneiform tablet through the post. The letters were easy for him to decipher - but not the words, which were in Arzawan, a mystery language known only from one or two Egyptian records. No one had yet been able to translate Arzawan, so Professor Winckler was intrigued. He decided to investigate the source of the tablet, a village called Boğazkale to the east of Ankara.

Professor Winckler was a wonderfully repellent character and cared little for appearances. He arrived in Boğazkale on 18 October 1905, after five days on horseback from Ankara, moaning all the way. But as soon as he arrived his mood improved out of all recognition. He found cuneiform tablets scattered all over the village and, just beyond the village limits, the remains of an ancient city. Massive stone walls girded a hill above a river and there was a large entrance gate guarded by stone lions.

Winckler's subsequent excavations revealed a palace at the heart of an ancient city. Inside the palace was one of the earliest libraries ever uncovered - the remains of hundreds upon hundreds of tablets, mostly in Arzawan, which had once been neatly arranged on wooden shelves with careful lists showing what was where.

When Arzawan was finally deciphered in 1906, a further surprise was in store. Until then, it had been assumed that the shadowy Hittites, about whom almost nothing was known, spoke a middle-eastern language, perhaps related to the semitic languages spoken in Palestine and Mesopotamia. It turned out that Hittite/Arzawan was an 'Indo-European' language, related to early European languages. And the Hittites, no longer shadowy, had once been so powerful that their rulers wrote on equal terms to the pharaohs of Ancient Egypt - which was why the first Arzawan text had been uncovered in Egypt.

Rich as Croesus

The Hittites were overcome by various invaders around 1180 BC. After a period of instability, a new power centre was established by a people, called the Phrygians, from slightly further north, under their King Midas in 750 BC. The Phrygians are famous for having invented embroidery and for the 'Phrygian Cap' worn by French revolutionaries when guillotining aristocrats thousands of years later. Their capital was Gordium, about 100 kilometres to the west of Ankara.

After the Phrygians came the Lydians, who probably spoke a language related to ancient Hittite. The Lydians were a gifted people. They invented gold and silver coinage, thus starting a revolution in trade which helped them to become extremely wealthy. Croesus was their last king. He was so rich that the saying 'rich as Croesus' is still used today. He was defeated by the Persians in 546 BC.

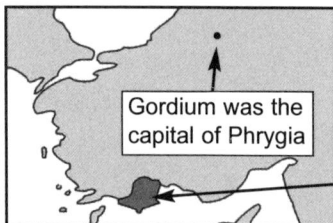

Gordium was the capital of Phrygia

People speaking Hittite, or related languages, continued to live in scattered kingdoms such as Lycia.

GREEKS AND ROMANS
HELLENISM

In Brief - from Alexander to Constantine

334 BC	Alexander the Great crosses the Hellespont.
41 BC	Mark Antony in Tarsus.
AD 10	Saint Paul born in Tarsus.
AD 323	Emperor Constantine becomes sole Roman Emperor.
AD 324	Christianity becomes a state religion of the Roman Empire
AD 330	Constantinople founded.

Alexander the Great

In the spring of 334 BC, Alexander the Great, then just twenty-two years old, crossed the Hellespont (the Dardanelles) from Europe into Anatolia with an army of 32,000 Greek infantry and 5,100 cavalry. His aim was to throw the Persians, then the ruling power in the region, out of Anatolia.

Alexander was a passionate believer in the superiority of Greek culture. On all his campaigns he carried with him a copy of the *Iliad* by Homer, greatest of Greek poets. The *Iliad* describes a war between heroes from the Greek mainland and the inhabitants of the city of Troy in Anatolia which probably took place around 1,250 BC. The war ends with the capture of Troy by means of a hollow, wooden horse.

Leaving his army to complete the crossing of the Hellespont, Alexander sailed south with some close companions for a brief visit to the site of ancient Troy, then already a ruin. Ever the tourist, he sacrificed at the tomb of the legendary Greek hero Achilles, anointed himself with oil and together with his friends raced naked round Achilles's tomb, in honour of the ancient hero. He then returned to his army.

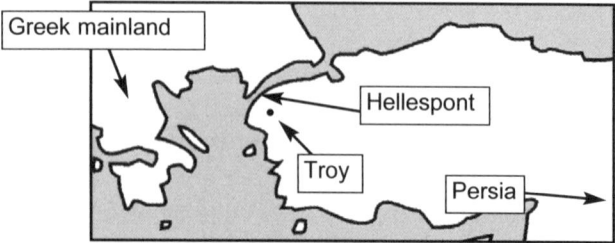

If you're in Cannakale
The site of ancient Troy lies thirty kilometers to the south of Cannakale where it dominates a wide plain. It's open to visitors and comes complete with a vast wooden horse.

Western Anatolia, which the Greeks called Ionia, was far from being an alien, foreign land to Alexander and his Greek soldiers when they invaded in 334 BC. This region had been an important part of Greek culture for centuries. Greek city-states were strung along the Mediterranean and Black Sea coasts of Anatolia like beads on a necklace. It was in these states rather than on the Greek mainland that the first flowering of classical Greek culture took place.

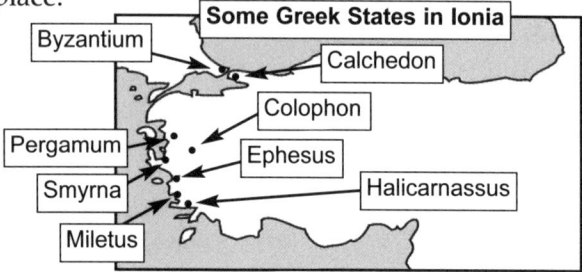

Greek Greats of Anatolia

Homer was said by some to have come from Smyrna (modern Izmir).

Thales (*c*.624 - 547 BC) was the father of Greek philosophy. He lived in Miletus and taught that water is the fundamental component of the universe. Not much of a theory by modern standards, but the first attempt to explain the world by reasoning rather than by religious myth.

Anaximander (610-546/5 BC), also from Miletus, was the first person to establish that the surface of the Earth is curved. He also claimed that life started in the sea, an astonishing foresight considering modern ideas of evolution.

Xenophanes (born *c*.570 BC), from Colophon, north west of the Ephesus, was an early free thinker, famous for his statement: 'If donkeys could speak, they would describe God as a super-donkey'.

Heraclitus (*c*.540-480 BC) came from Ephesus. He reasoned that the basic element of the universe is fire and that all things are in a constant state of flux, as illustrated by his statement: 'one cannot step into the same river twice'.

A knotty problem

Alexander defeated the Persians at the Battle of Granicus (modern Kocabas) a little to the east of Troy, then liberated the Greek cities of the coast from Persian rule. By the spring of 333 BC he was ready to turn inland, to Gordium, ancient capital of the Phrygians.

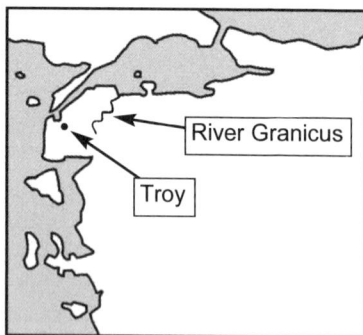

At Gordium, Alexander, always a compulsive sightseer, examined the chariot of the ancient Phrygian King Gordius, founder of the city. The yoke of this famous relic was attached to its pole by a complicated knot. Legend had it that whoever untied the knot would go on to conquer Asia. Alexander fiddled with the knot for a few minutes, realised that the task was hopeless and drew his sword, slashing the knot in two thus creating a saying: 'to cut the Gordian knot'. Later that year he and his army left Anatolia via the Cilician Gates. He went on to conquer the rest of the Persian Empire, including Mesopotamia, Syria, Palestine and Egypt - the entire 'known' world.

If you're near Adana or Tarsus

The Cilician Gates enter their narrowest point in a gorge where the River Gökoluk cuts through the Taurus Mountains. The main road from Ankara to Adana bypasses the gorge a little to the west but the old road is still there and it's pretty spectacular. Alternatively, the train line lies a little to the east. This is the old Baghdad Railway line, begun by the Germans in 1904 and a superb feat of engineering. It was intended as a strategic short cut to India and as such it was a threat to the then British Empire.

Having conquered pretty well everyone, Alexander died in Babylon on 11 June 323 BC, after a prolonged drinking bout. His huge empire was broken up among his top generals.

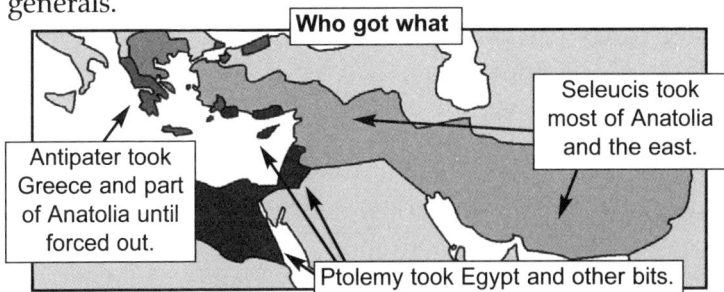

Who got what

Seleucis took most of Anatolia and the east.

Antipater took Greece and part of Anatolia until forced out.

Ptolemy took Egypt and other bits.

If you're traveling west from Ankara

Gordion or Gordium, the capital of the ancient Phrygians, lies 106 kilometres west of Ankara. The city was destroyed several times over the centuries but the remains of four 'great houses' are still visible. The area around the city is littered with the remains of over a hundred Phrygian royal tombs. The largest of these, the 'mound of Midas', is open to the public. It's an enormous tumulus about 300 metres in diameter and 43 metres high. When first excavated it was found to contain the remains of a man over sixty years old as well as funeral objects.

Breasts

The Temple of Diana at Ephesus (modern Efes) was one of the Seven Wonders of the ancient world. It covered twice the area of the Parthenon at Athens, it had 127 columns, each towering eighteen metres above the marble floor and it was built on swampy ground, on a bed of charcoal and fleeces of wool to protect it against earthquakes. Pilgrims and tourists came from far and wide to pay homage.

But none saw the goddess. Diana of Ephesus was always heavily veiled. Only her priests were allowed to see her

23

image, a gnarled, wooden statue with many breasts. She was immensely old, known to the Romans as Diana, to the Greeks as Artemis, to the Phrygians as Cybele, to the Hittites as Kubaba and known as heaven-knows-what before that. She was the ancient mother-goddess of Anatolia. In Phrygian times and perhaps earlier, the ecstatic ceremonies of her 'Day of Blood' might climax in the self-castration of male devotees.

After Alexander's death, the goddess Diana presided over a world which was overwhelmingly Greek. Hellenistic (Greek) culture was all-powerful, rather as Western culture has been recently. To be Hellenistic was to be modern. In the Hellenistic period, cities such as Ephesus expanded rapidly. At its peak Ephesus had a population of over 200,000 and Pergamum further up the coast (modern Bergama) was only slightly smaller. And these great cities were still small compared to the great centres of Antioch (population 350,000) and Alexandria (population 500,000-700,000). Non-Greek cities also followed Greek fashions and built baths, theatres and temples in the Greek style. This Greek-dominated world stretched from the Middle East across the Mediterranean shore.

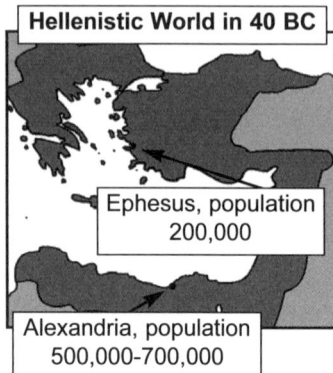

Hellenistic World in 40 BC

Ephesus, population 200,000

Alexandria, population 500,000-700,000

She was gorgeous

By 41 BC, nearly three hundred years after Alexander's death, the Hellenistic world was growing tired. A new and more ruthless power threatened to take over. That year, when a Roman general called Mark Antony arrived in

Hellenistic Ephesus, he was greeted as a conquering hero by the town's Greek citizens rather than being looked down on as a foreigner - the usual ancient-Greek attitude towards lesser mortals. In fact the citizens dressed up festively as Greek mythical beasts to mark the occasion.

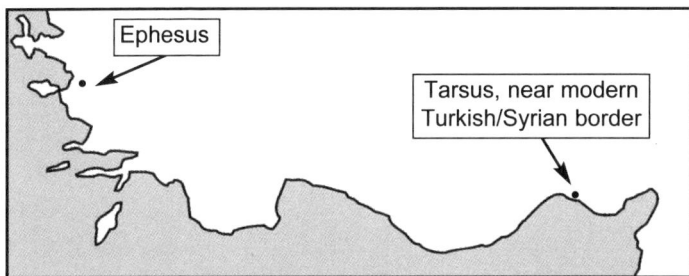

Antony worshipped at the Temple of Diana and then proceeded south to the city of Tarsus and there, in the late summer of 41 BC, Cleopatra, Hellenistic Queen of Egypt, came to visit him. Her arrival was described by the Roman writer Plutarch in words later exploited by Shakespeare:

She sailed up the river Cydnus, in a barge with gilded stern and billowing sails of purple, while silver oars beat time to the music of flutes, fifes and harps. She herself lay under an awning of cloth of gold, dressed as Venus. Beautiful boys, like painted Cupids, stood on each side to fan her. Her maids were dressed as sea nymphs, some steered and others worked the ropes. Perfumes from her barge could be smelled along the shore, where huge crowds had gathered to watch her arrival ...

Cleopatra was bewitchingly beautiful. She was twenty-seven to Antony's forty-two, a funny, clever woman who could speak twelve languages. At the banquet which followed Antony was totally captivated. But Cleopatra for her part had good reason to turn on the charm. She'd not come to Tarsus voluntarily - Antony had summoned her. By 41 BC, it was Roman power which counted in the Hellenistic world and right then Antony was the most powerful commander in the Roman Empire having recently won a Roman civil war.

If you're in Tarsus

Tarsus was once an important trading centre. Goods brought down from the Taurus mountains through the Cilician Gates were loaded onto ships in the harbour below the city, for onward shipment to Egypt and the Middle East. The River Cydnus, which once connected the city to the sea, was diverted in the sixth century and the original water course is now silted up. It's no longer possible to see exactly where Cleopatra would have sailed her perfumed barge but the remains of a Roman gate mark the main entrance between the city and the harbour so presumably she would have walked or been carried that way. The gate is called the 'Gate of Cleopatra' although there is no definite connection.

Constantine

The Roman conquest of the Hellenistic world was a gradual affair and was already well on its way by the time Antony met Cleopatra. Anatolia became part of the Roman Empire. It was carved up into a number of Roman client kingdoms and provinces, Tarsus being part of the province of Cilicia.

The ancient world, of which Anatolia was such an important part, was changing fast and it was about to change beyond all imagining. Jesus Christ was born a bit to the south in Palestine, perhaps about thirty-two years after Mark Antony's meeting with Cleopatra. His followers, originally an obscure Jewish sect, differed from other Jewish sects in that they decided to convert non-Jews to Judaism. From very early on, the Christian Church was part of Hellenistic/Roman culture. The very earliest Christian texts, the biblical letters of Saint Paul, were written in Greek to Christian communities in various Hellenistic cities of the first century. Paul, described as a small man with thinning hair and joined-up eyebrows, was himself a native of Tarsus, born around AD 10.

Soon there were converts throughout the Roman Empire including many in Anatolia where some of the very earliest Christian communities took root in cities such as Ephesus and Tarsus. Despite persecution, the sect grew larger and larger. Finally, in AD 312, the Roman Emperor Constantine (c.274-337), who was himself a Christian sympathiser, seized power, becoming sole ruler in 323.

The new religion had reached the very top.

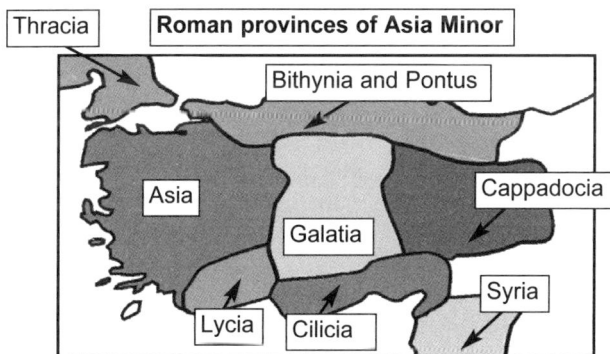

Thracia — Roman provinces of Asia Minor — Bithynia and Pontus — Asia — Galatia — Cappadocia — Lycia — Cilicia — Syria

Constantinople
Seven years after he came to power, Constantine, now 'the Great', founded the city of Constantinople (modern

Istanbul) as a new, Christian capital for the Roman Empire (AD 330). At the heart of this new city was the *Milion*, the first milestone. From this spot all distances in the Empire were to be measured. Over the *Milion* was a dome supported on four open arches and above the dome was set the holiest of all Christians relics - the True Cross on which Christ had been crucified (*c.* AD 30). The message was clear: Christianity was now at the very heart of the Roman Empire.

And that heart was in Anatolia/Thrace.

If you're in Istanbul

All that remains of the *Milion* is the 'First Mile Post' a marble stone jutting from the ground at the north-eastern end of Sultanahmet Square near the entrance to the underground Basilica cistern, which was built by the Emperor Justinian in AD 532.

THE JEWEL OF THE WORLD

THE BYZANTINES

In brief - the Byzantine Empire (all AD)	
323-337	Constantine the Great
361-363	Julian the Apostate
379-395	Theodoric I
408-450	Theodoric II (built the walls)
527-565	Justinian (and Theodora)
537	Haghia Sophia rebuilt
610-641	Heraclius
867-1028	Golden Age of the Macedonian dynasty
1204-1261	Crusader kings in charge
1261-1453	Long decline

Byzas lives

Constantinople was built over a small Greek town called Byzantium, founded in 667 BC and named after its founder, the legendary Byzas. What was once a small, local colony was transformed in a short space of time into a vast city. But although Byzantium disappeared under Constantine's vast new building works, its name lived on. The late, eastern Roman Empire, ruled from Constantinople, became known as the 'Byzantine Empire'.

A throne fit for an emperor

In AD 392, the Roman Empire was divided in two (for the second time) by Emperor Theodoric the Great. The western half was to be ruled from Rome, the eastern, Byzantine half continued to be ruled from Constantinople. The western half crumbled - it fell to barbaric German tribes in the fifth century AD - but in the east, in

Constantinople, the Empire continued in all its glory for hundreds more years, a beacon of civilisation through the Dark Ages of Europe and the Middle East.

To visitors from lesser lands the Byzantine Empire seemed dazzlingly rich and powerful. The throne room of the palace at Constantinople was quite incredible. Visiting dignitaries would gasp in amazement when first they entered. Around the room, mechanical birds sang mechanical songs from perches in artificial trees. At the far end, on either side of the Emperor on his gold and bronze throne, mechanical lions roared and swished their mechanical tails. It took a moment to realise that the lions weren't real either. It was customary for the dignitaries to prostrate themselves three times before the throne. On rising, they saw that the throne, which had stood on a low platform when they last looked, had now risen miraculously towards the ceiling and the Emperor gazed down on them, bathed in brilliant light like a god.

Constantinople

Constantinople was the mightiest city in the world with a population of between 500,000 and a million in the sixth century. A Chinese traveller, writing of the marvels of 'Fu Lin', described buildings decorated with gold, ivory and crystal, innumerable churches, water-powered machines, fountains and a mechanical man made of gold which marked the hours by striking bells. The city was also a museum. Constantine had crammed it with treasures from all over the ancient world: a stone column from Ancient Egypt, a column from the Temple of Apollo in Delphi in Ancient Greece, a figure of the goddess Athene from Troy where once Alexander had run naked, the True Cross of Christ, the hatchet used by Noah to build the Ark and many, many other relics. Meanwhile the city spilled out beyond its original walls. Beginning in 413 during the reign of the Emperor Theodoric II, new walls were built to protect the new suburbs. These are the mighty Theodosian Walls, finally breached by Sultan Mehmet in 1453, whose massive ruins can still be seen today.

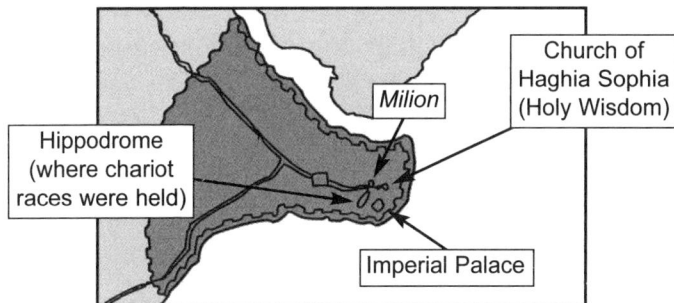

Justinian and Theodora

In many ways Constantinople was weirdly different from any modern city but in some ways it was surprisingly similar. A modern football fan would have had no trouble understanding it. In Byzantine times, the population of Constantinople was divided into two factions, the Blues and the Greens. Each colour supported a different chariot team at the Hippodrome and their support was fanatical. In the 520s the Blues were dominant. Blue thugs of the period wore their hair long at the back and short at the front with long moustaches and beards in the style of the barbarian Huns. Bunches of them, armed to the teeth, patrolled the streets robbing passers-by at will. Greens kept their heads down.

The Empress Theodora (c.497-548) began life as the daughter of a bear-keeper to the Greens. (Bear fights were part of the entertainment at the Hippodrome.) When her father died, the Greens gave the bear-keeping job to a stranger, leaving Theodora's mother and young children in poverty, and it was the Blues who rescued them. So

Theodora became a Blue and it was probably through the Blues that she met her future husband Justinian.

Justinian (527-565) was the Emperor's nephew and the second most powerful man in the Empire when he met Theodora. He backed the Blues for political rather than sentimental reasons, because they were the most powerful group in the capital after the army. When they met, Theodora was quite a well-known comic actress. Her morals were possibly not of the highest and her act seems to have included the odd bit of striptease but she was very clever and very beautiful and Justinian fell passionately in love. In 527, he became Emperor and Theodora, the bear-keeper's daughter, became his Empress.

They were the most famous imperial couple in all the long history of Byzantium.

Haghia Sophia

In January 532, in the early years of Justinian's reign, the Blues and the Greens united and turned on the new Emperor in protest at the punishment of some rowdy supporters from both factions. Crowds poured out of the Hippodrome and set fire to the gateway of the Imperial Palace. From there the flames spread to the church of Haghia Sophia next door, burning it to the ground. Justinian appeared in the royal box at the Hippodrome and pleaded for order but he was shouted down. Turning from riot to revolution, the mob acclaimed an elderly general, Hypatius, as the new Emperor, crowning him with a gold necklace lent by an onlooker.

Justinian's life was now in danger. He and some close advisers retired to a room behind the royal box. His great general Belisarius, who was part of the royal party, attempted to re-enter the Hippodrome but was forced back almost immediately. The situation was now desperate. A private galley* was moored in the harbour of the Palace and there was a direct corridor between Palace and Hippodrome. Justinian decided to make a run for it.

It was at this point that Theodora intervened.

If you, my lord, want to save your skin, you can easily do so. We are rich, there is the sea, and there too are our ships. But think first whether, after you reach safety, you will not regret that you did not choose death instead. As for me - purple** is the noblest shroud ...

How could the men flee when a woman showed such courage? Fortunately, at this point, Blues and Greens reverted to type and started killing each other. Belisarius and another general went round by the Palace, gathered some Imperial troops and stormed back into the Hippodrome. 30,000 Blues and Greens lay dead before the end of the day.

*A galley was a low fast vessel propelled by sails and banks of oars.
**Purple was the imperial colour. Emperors wore it and even their coffins were draped in it. Empresses gave birth to their children in a purple room in the palace. Emperors directly descended in the royal line in this way were said to be *Porphyrogenitos* - 'born in the purple'.

Justinian survived to reign for thirty-eight years. He pushed the frontiers of the Empire as far as Spain. But his greatest achievement was the new church of Haghia Sophia (Holy Wisdom). It was designed by the Greek mathematician Anthemius of Tralles and the engineer Isidore of Miletus and it was the largest building in the world until the completion of Saint Peter's in Rome in the sixteenth century. The walls were faced in rare marbles collected from around the empire and beyond and the ceilings glittered with fabulous mosaics. The dome, rebuilt in 562 after an earthquake, soared, and still soars, sixty-two metres above the ground.

When Haghia Sophia was completed in 537 and Justinian saw the interior without its scaffolding for the first time, he stood for several minutes in stunned silence. Finding his voice, he said at last:

Solomon, I have surpassed thee.

Islam

For hundreds of years the Byzantine Empire was the dominant power in Anatolia and Thrace and far beyond. It's only real competitor was the Persian Empire to the east. In September 628 the Emperor Heraclius returned to Constantinople having defeated the Persians and saved the Empire from almost certain collapse after it had been reduced to a terrible state under the previous Emperor, a bad egg called Phocas. The whole city had turned out to greet Heraclius waving olive branches, the symbol of peace. On the final stretch of his triumphal progress towards the Palace, the streets were strewn ankle-deep in rose petals.

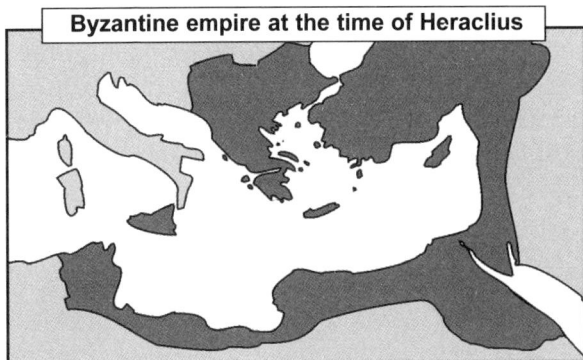

Byzantine empire at the time of Heraclius

Heraclius was a true hero. He achieved his decisive victory over the Persians in 627, killing three Persian generals personally in single combat. But that same year, an obscure Arab leader by the name of Mohammed was leading his followers in a local skirmish near his home town of Mecca in the Arabian Peninsula. Neither Heraclius nor the Persian Emperor could have had any idea that this obscure Arab, if they even heard about him, was a greater threat to both than either of them was to the other.

Mohammed was born in 570, five years before Heraclius. He died in 632. His new religion fired his followers with extraordinary confidence, confidence which resulted in extraordinary military success and ultimately in the destruction of the Byzantine Empire, although that finally happened hundreds of years later.

In 635 the Muslims captured Jerusalem and in 636 they defeated Heraclius himself at the Battle of Yarmouk. The Byzantines were driven back into their Anatolian heartland with the Arabs in hot pursuit. Three times, Arab armies trudged across Anatolia to Constantinople while their ships went round by sea, but they never took Constantinople itself. In 669 and 674-78 and again in 716-17, they were driven off.

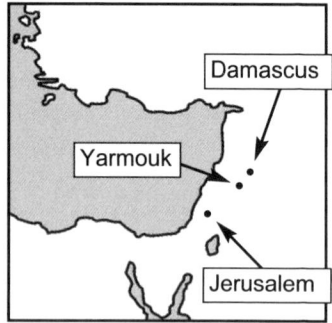

Greek Fire

The most dangerous of the Arab attacks on Constantinople were the repeated attacks of 674-78. What tipped the scales in favour of the Byzantines was a new invention - 'Greek Fire', first used in 674. Greek Fire was ideal against ships as it was a sort of oily chemical which burned when in contact with water - no one now knows the recipe. It could be fired from catapults or forced from a pump under pressure. Supposedly, it was invented by an unnamed Syrian architect and a Greek mechanic called Callinicus.

In Brief - early Muslim advances

c.570   Birth of Mohammed
c.575   Birth of Heraclius
635   Muslims capture Jerusalem
636   Battle of Yarmouk
669   First Muslim attack on
         Constantinople

Manzikert and the Turks

In spite of the Arabs, the Byzantines were a force to be reckoned with until well into the eleventh century. Then in 1071, at the Battle of Manzikert in eastern Anatolia, the

Byzantine Emperor Romanus IV (1067-81) was defeated by a new enemy - the Turks. The Turks were nomads from central Asia who had established themselves as soldiers of the Islamic Caliph (means 'Successor' - eg he who succeeds Mohammed as leader of the Muslim Faithful) in Baghdad. They were recent converts to Islam and fanatical warriors. After the Battle of Manzikert, the eastern border of Anatolia lay wide open to them. By 1200, much of Anatolia had turned into a patchwork of small Turkish statelets and Byzantium had been reduced to a shadow of its former self.

If you're near Lake Van

The precise location of the Battle of Manzikert is uncertain. Probably it took place on a level steppe about two kilometers from the fortress of Manzikert, in the modern town of Malazgirt about forty miles north of Lake Van. The steppe is bordered by rough, hill country. The Byzantine cavalry were lured into following the Turkish horsemen into the hills where the Turks had prepared an ambush. The Byzantine infantry were unable to come to the aid of their cavalry and eventually the Emperor Romanus ordered the imperial standards to be reversed, which was the order to retreat. At this point the Turks charged forwards and the Byzantines were routed. It was the worst defeat in Byzantine history and was referred to ever afterwards as 'That Terrible Day'.

Golden Nose

Byzantine rulers used blinding, tongue-cutting and nose-cutting to subdue their opponents as an alternative to killing them. The Emperor Justinian Rhinometus (ruled 685-95) was a victim of nose-cutting - *Rhinometus* means cut-nose. In later life he wore a gold replacement.

The end already

Manzikert was the beginning of the end for the Byzantines, but the end took a long time coming - another 382 years to be precise. The next really big disaster for Byzantium wasn't caused by the Turks, not directly anyway, but by fellow Christians.

The Crusaders, medieval Christian warriors from western Europe, were every bit as fanatical as their Muslim opponents. Starting in the eleventh century they trudged repeatedly across Europe and into Asia with the intention of recapturing Jerusalem from the Turks who by then were in control of the Holy Land.

The First Crusade (1095-99) was victorious.
The Second Crusade was a failure.
The Third Crusade was a draw.
The Fourth Crusade (1202-04) was a disaster - for the Byzantines.

All the Crusades were worrying for the Byzantines. The

trick was how to get these foreign armies across Byzantine territory before they did too much damage. There was no love lost between eastern and western Christians. To the Byzantines, the Roman Catholic Crusaders were boorish thugs; to the Crusaders, the Greek-speaking Byzantines were devious heretics. In 1204 the knights of the Fourth Crusade turned on their Byzantine hosts and sacked Constantinople. During an orgy of destruction, drunken Crusaders placed a prostitute on the throne of the Patriarch, the leader of the Greek Church, beside the high altar in Haghia Sophia, and danced round her jeering and singing. The treasures of a thousand years were either stolen or destroyed. From 1204-61, Constantinople was ruled by western thugs. The Byzantine Empire never really recovered from the shock.

WILD HORSEMEN
THE TURKS

In Brief	
1055	Tughril Beg seizes control of Baghdad.
1071	Battle of Manzikert
1320s	Osman seizes Bithynia
1354	Turks reach Europe
1365	Janissaries founded
1389	Battle of 'Blackbird Field'.
1402	Battle of Ankara - Beyazit defeated by Tamerlane
1453	Turks take Constantinople.

Pony tales

Horses were first tamed somewhere out on the great grasslands of eastern Europe and central Asia around five thousand years ago. It was from this same area that the Turks first galloped into history in the 800s.

The early Turks fought on horseback and their method of fighting was highly mobile. On their small, tough ponies, they could cover up to a hundred and fifty miles in a day if they had to, at a time when thirty miles was considered reasonable going. They were superb warriors. They could shoot backwards at full gallop at a moving target, many arrows to the minute. The ponies were almost as impressive as the riders. Their tails were dyed red. They were very intelligent and easily trained - one of their useful tricks was to pick up a sword from the ground with their teeth and pass it to the rider.

Archery

Sultan Selim the Sot, or Selim the Fair to his hangers-on (reigned 1566-74), was no warrior and took no interest in government. He was a plump man who loved wine. He drank it by the litre.

But military skills ran deep. When not drunk, even this less-than warlike Turkish sultan could bring down a skylark on the wing with his bow and arrow - so it's said.

Seljuks

The early Turks were employed as slave or mercenary soldiers by the rulers of the Islamic world. They were the toughest soldiers around so they were much in demand. By AD 840 the Caliph in Baghdad had a Turkish bodyguard.

It was the old story - civilised leader employs barbarian soldiers, barbarian soldiers get uppity, barbarian soldiers take over. By 1055 a Turkish leader called Tughril Beg had seized control of Baghdad, if only briefly, and the Caliph was his puppet. Tughril carved out an empire south of the Caspian Sea.

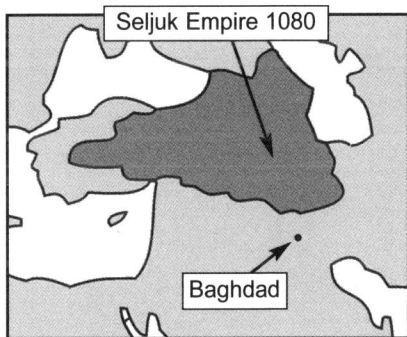

Seljuk Empire 1080

Baghdad

Tughril Beg, the grandson of a leader called Seljuk, a member of the Ghuzz tribe of Turks, was the first leader of the Seljuk dynasty of Turks. Next to rule was his nephew Alp Arslan (Brave Lion) and he was the leader who

41

defeated the Byzantine Emperor Romanus IV at the Battle of Manzikert in 1071. From then on, the Turks pushed deeper and deeper into Anatolia, until 1243 when they were defeated by meaner, nastier nomads from the east - by the Mongols.

Ottomans

After 1243 and their defeat by the Mongols, the Seljuks were a spent force. The next big Turkish ruler was Osman (or Othman) I (1300-26), founder of the Ottoman dynasty, who started his career as a simple commander, or *bey*. He was a Turk of the old school. He dressed simply, ate with his men and saw to the shoeing of his own horses. He was such a good commander that men came flocking to follow his horsetail standard, not just Turks but impoverished Byzantine peasants, runaway slaves and other adventurers. In the 1320s, he seized most of the province of Bithynia and his ships were soon raiding Christian shipping on the Sea of Marmara.

In Brief

The Ottoman dynasty took up where the Seljuks had left off. Under the Ottomans the Turks flourished as never before:

1327	Fall of the Byzantine city of Bursa.
1329	Ancient Nicaea falls to the Ottomans.
1346	Ottoman troops under Orkhan cross the Dardenelles into Europe.
1361	Orkhan's son, Murad I takes the Thracian capital Adrianople (Edirne).

In the space of just fifty years, the Byzantine Empire was reduced to a fraction of its former size and surrounded by a powerful Turkish state.

Janissaries

Murad I, grandson of Osman, was a big man with a big nose. Not for him the simple title of *bey*, nor even *emir* which meant 'chief'. Murad was the first of the Ottomans to call himself *Sultan*, meaning 'sovereign'. He set up the much of the early Ottoman machinery of government. This included, among other things, the office of chief minister or 'grand Vizier' (literally 'Sultan's foot'), the *devsirme* or 'child-tribute' - and the Janissaries.

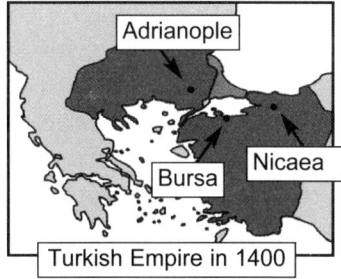

Turkish Empire in 1400

Every three years a collector would tour the Christian villages of Greece and the Balkans, and also Christian villages in Anatolia. He would select the finest Christian youths to be slaves of the sultan. There was little stigma attached to being the sultan's slave taken in the *devsirme*. Slaves of the sultan lived far better than those who remained to scratch a living on the home farm. However, that having been said, the collections must have hurt the families who were left behind.

The tribute boys were brought up as Muslims. The brightest of them were educated at the palace schools and went on to be viziers and other high officers of the Empire. The rest were trained to be soldiers of the *jani ceri*, the 'new troop', (founded 1365). Selected for physical perfection, the Janissaries, in their red boots and white linen hats were the best and strongest soldiers in the Empire - and in Europe. They formed the backbone of the regular army along with the *spahi*, the best of the Turkish cavalry on their tough, red-tailed ponies. It was a clever and fearful system. In the words of Sultan Mehmet:

43

We light our lamp with oil taken from the hearts of the infidels.

The Thunderbolt and strangulation of brothers

Under Osman's son Orkhan and then under his grandson Murad I, the Turkish advance continued. They struck deeper and deeper into Christian Europe. Then in 1389, Murad I led an army into the Balkans. At Kosovo Polje, the 'Blackbird Field', he was met by a Christian Serb army led by Prince, later Saint, Lazar. During the battle which followed, Lazar's son-in-law, a warrior by the name of Milosh Obravitch, talked his way into Murad's tent by pretending to be a deserter. He stabbed Murad with a poisoned dagger. Murad's eldest son, Beyazit, took over command and won the battle.

Beyazit, known as *Yilderim* ('the Thunderbolt') was the son of Murad and a Byzantine princess. He was a brutal man and a born fighter. Immediately the battle was over he ordered the strangulation of his younger brother in order to remove any challenge to his authority, thus starting the appalling tradition of fratricide whereby new sultans wiped out all their male siblings on coming to the throne. Beyazit extended the Turkish Empire to include most of Anatolia and the Balkans.

In 1402 Beyazit turned towards the east. He took on the Mongol conqueror Timur Lenk as the Turks called him, or 'Tamerlane' as he's known in English. Tamerlane had carved out a vast empire for himself in central Asia and was starting to put pressure on the eastern frontiers of the Ottomans. The two warlords met at the Battle of Ankara (1402) and Beyazit lost. He was taken prisoner. Tamerlane treated him well until Beyazit's prickly personality became too much of a nuisance. Beyazit was forced into a cage which was too small to stand up in and dragged behind Tamerlane's entourage. His wife was forced to serve naked at Tamerlane's table. After several weeks of this torture Beyazit beat his brains out on the bars of his cage.

War machine

Tamurlane's victory stemmed the Ottoman tide but it didn't stop it. After a brief interval, the Ottoman conquests continued under Beyazit's son Mehmet I and his grandson Murad II.

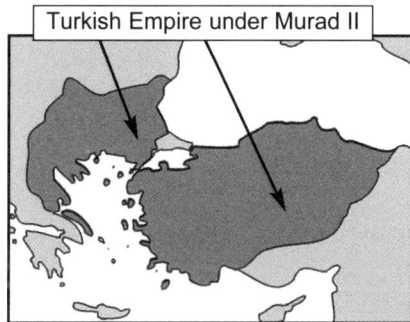

Turkish Empire under Murad II

The Ottoman state was a war machine pure and simple. It had to keep expanding or it would fade away. For five months of the year, the regular army stayed in camp but every April the campaigning season started again and the army stirred itself for the next thrust into Christendom. Men came from all over Anatolia. They came not for pay but in search of booty and hoping that their courage and skill would win them a place in the ranks of the paid regulars.

The system of conquest was self-financing. The sultan awarded revenue from newly-conquered territory to his soldiers in lieu of pay. A cavalryman might be paid with a *timar*, the taxes from a small village, a commander might get a *ziamet*, the income from several villages. The *timar* system allowed the Turkish sultan to gather a far larger army in a far shorter space of time than any other ruler of his period - Christendom didn't stand a chance.

There were other advantages to the *timar* system - for the Turks and for the people they conquered. The soldiers who were given *timars* never owned the land or the village, they just received its taxes, thus no class of landed gentry ever had the chance to develop. On the other side of the equation, the peasants who paid the *timar* found themselves less heavily taxed than they had been previously by their Christian lords. Typically a Balkan peasant might be expected to give two days free labour per week to his Christian lord - but only about ten days per year to the Turks.

Faced by this relentless Ottoman war machine and by the undeniable attraction of Ottoman rule to many Byzantine subjects, the Byzantine Empire slowly crumbled away. By the 1450s, it had been reduced to a small island in a Turkish sea. Stripped of its great empire, pillaged by crusaders, its trade mainly in the hands of Italian merchants, Constantinople, the Byzantine capital, became a shell. The great walls still stood but behind them large tracts of land were empty or given over to allotments.

It was this shell of a city which Mehmet II, the Conqueror (1451-81), great-grandson of Beyazit, captured in 1453.

Revival

Mehmet the Conqueror was shocked by the desolate state of Constantinople in 1453 and set about reviving it. Captives from the siege were released and resettled within the walls and, from then on, wherever his conquests took him, his share of the captives was always marched back to Constantinople to settle there.

It was the Turkish capital now, but the Turks were tolerant. Everyone was allowed to practise his or her own religion, whether Catholic, Armenian, Greek Orthodox or Jewish. And as the Turkish Empire spread out into the Mediterranean, the Turks were often welcomed by the peasants as better overlords than the Catholic Venetians who controlled much of the eastern Mediterranean at that time. 'Better the sultan's turban than the bishop's mitre' was a common saying. Members of each religion were organised into separate groups or '*millets*'. The *millets* were left alone to run their own affairs so long as they paid the tax due from non-Muslims and kept out of mischief.

Of all the sects, it was the Greeks who predominated. In Constantinople, thirty-six churches were reserved for their use. When visiting the Greek Patriarch, the leader of the Greek Orthodox Church, Mehmet would never set foot inside the church, not because it was an infidel house of worship but because, if he had, it might have been claimed by Muslims as a sacred place and thus turned into a mosque, which was the last thing he wanted. Much better to attract tax-paying Greek citizens than to scare them off in such a way. The Patriarch was even given three horsetails as a symbol of his authority and thus incorporated into the Turkish power structure.

Selim the Grim

Mehmet followed up the capture of Constantinople with the conquest of most of the Greek world. And the tide of conquest continued under his successors. By the time Sultan Selim the Grim, his grandson, died of an infected boil in 1520, Egypt, Syria, Palestine and part of Iran had all been swallowed up, and the whole of the Middle East was now part of the Turkish Empire as well as most of the Balkans.

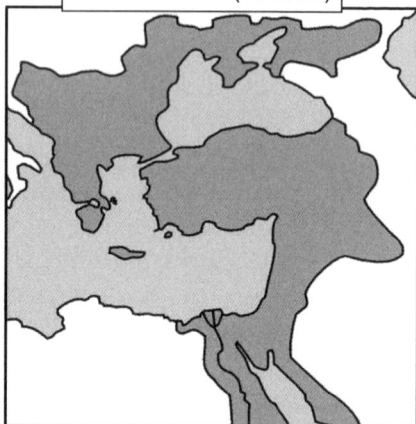

Turkish Empire at the time of the conquests of Selim the Grim (1512-21)

Selim the Grim's nickname was well earned. He was the third son of Beyazit II and was chosen by Beyazit to succeed him because of his courage and ruthless ambition. On the death of Beyazit in 1512, Selim eliminated both his elder brothers by having them strangled, thus continuing a royal tradition of fratricide. The five sons of his brothers, the youngest only five years old, he also had strangled. While the strangling was going on he listened to their cries from an adjoining room. As if this wasn't enough, he also beheaded seven Grand Viziers during the course of his reign. The phrase, 'May you become Selim's

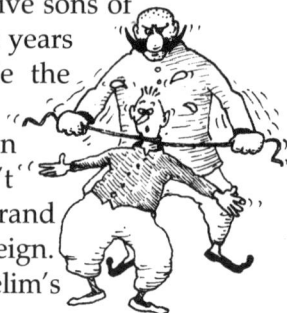

Vizier!' entered the language as a Turkish version of 'Go to hell!'.

Deaf mutes

A squad of muscular deaf mutes was used for the execution of important people. Members of the squad had their tongues slit and their ear drums pierced on the basis of 'hear no evil, speak no evil'. The weapon they used was a bowstring, a silken bowstring in the case of royal relatives and men of very high rank. After strangulation, the victim's head was severed from his body and sent to the sultan in a velvet bag. A yet more distinguished form of death was crushing of the testicles, a method used on Sultan Osman II in 1622.

SULEIMAN THE MAGNIFICENT

AND THE SULTANATE OF WOMEN

In Brief	
1520	Suleiman the Magnificent becomes sultan
1523	Roxelana joins the Harem
1529	First attack on Vienna
1536	Ibrahim strangled
1566	Death of Suleiman

Silence please

The Ottoman Empire at the height of its power was unlike any other empire. It was simultaneously modest and extravagant. A visitor waiting in the second courtyard of the Topkapi Palace in Constantinople might be forgiven feelings of confusion. It wasn't a grand place by palatial standards elsewhere. The surrounding buildings were low. But it was unnerving nevertheless. At first glance it seemed to be lined with sculptures, at second glance the visitor realised that these weren't sculptures at all. They were living men who stood absolutely motionless and in utter silence.

Stillness and silence. This palace perched on a beautiful promontory above the Bosphorus and the Sea of Marmara, at the heart of one of the biggest cities in the world, was the calm at the centre of the Turkish storm. In the innermost court no one spoke unless ordered to and even sneezing and coughing were prohibited. From the 1520s, attendants communicated in *ixarette*, a sign language for the deaf and dumb.

The Turkish sultan's ability to impose silence was an expression of his absolute power. Outside the Palace he moved in an envelope of calm. A soft, short murmur was all the greeting he received or wanted from the crowds which lined his route as he made his way to the mosque (previously the great church) of Haghia Sophia on Fridays or out to join his army in the spring. Even on campaign, the silence followed him. The camps of the Ottoman army were very different to the noisy, drunken camps of their Christian enemies. No sounds louder than the jingling of horses' harness or the clang of cooking pots being unpacked ready for cooking disturbed the general sense of good order.

Vienna - first time around

In mid-September 1529, the sky to the south-east of Vienna was marked by a few, slender columns of smoke rising lazily towards grey, moisture-laden clouds - smoke from villages burnt by outriders of the Turkish army, terrifying first sign of the Turkish approach. Gradually the fires grew closer, preceded by waves of terrified refugees heading for the shelter of the city. Then the advance guard appeared, a vast multitude of men already far outnumbering the

Viennese defenders, and finally the main Turkish force which rapidly encircled the city, such a huge army that it seemed to stretch to the horizon in all directions.

The Viennese defenders watched helplessly while, beneath the walls, Turkish cavalrymen whooped and brandished their spears to the thunder of four hundred elephant drums and camel drums and the shrilling of double-reeded hautboys*. (It was the Turks who invented the military band.) On each cavalryman's spear was impaled the head of an Austrian victim. These advance cavalrymen were probably members of the *Deli* regiment, the regiment of madmen. The *Deli* men always rode at the front. They wore the outspread wings of black eagles on their helmets and tiger skins over their shoulders and they were utterly reckless of life - their own as well as other people's.

It was an alien and frightening force which appeared beneath the walls of Vienna that September day, deliberately so perhaps. At the heart of the Turkish army, as always, were the *spahis*, the Turkish cavalry, and the Janissary infantry drawn from the *devsirme*, the tribute of Christian slave boys. The Janissaries never marched in step but with an odd swaying motion. They were tough. They could go for weeks if they had to on a diet of flour, salt and spices. Not that they didn't like food - rather the opposite. The titles of their commanders were all food-related and were as alien as their uniforms: Soupmen, Head Scullions, Head Cooks, Head Water Carriers. The

*A hautboy is an early type of oboe.

emblem of each regiment was a six-foot soup ladle and a bronze cauldron. Loss of its cauldron was the greatest disgrace which could befall a regiment.

In 1529 the Turkish army consisted of around 300,000 men. Against them, there were just 20,000 defenders. The Austrians had had time to repair the walls, to dig additional earthworks, and to flatten the suburbs for a clear field of fire but despite these preparations they clearly didn't stand a chance, or they wouldn't have done without one crucial factor - the weather.

Early sixteenth-century Turkish artillery was far superior to western artillery in terms of firepower, but heavy rain and the subsequent mud had made it impossible to drag most of their heavy guns up from Constantinople. A trail of abandoned cannon marked their passage through the Balkans. In the siege which followed, the Turks were reduced to trying to undermine the city walls. After more than two weeks of ferocious fighting with horrific loss of life, they'd still failed to make headway and Sultan Suleiman the Magnificent decided that enough was enough. A last assault on 14 October was beaten off like all the others and on the 19th the Turkish army packed their bags and set off for home.

With hindsight, the first siege of Vienna marked the high tide of Turkish expansion. If Vienna had fallen in 1529, the Turks, then at the peak of their power, might well have gone on to conquer western Europe. And we also know that Suleiman's ambition stretched further still. He had in his possession a map drawn up for Christopher Columbus a mere thirty-seven years earlier.

It described part of the Atlantic coast of America.

Building works

Suleiman came to power in 1521. By 1529, when he ordered the withdrawal from Vienna, he already had a string of successes to his credit:

1521	Capture of Belgrade, the Serbian capital.
1523	Capture of Rhodes from the Crusader Knights of Saint John.
1526	Battle of Mohacs - decisive defeat of Hungary

The Turkish war machine was no longer invincible but it was still very efficient. Each year the armies set out from Constantinople and each year fresh tribute of slaves and money poured back into the capital. This wealth was reflected in a sumptuous building programme. Between 1540 and 1620, Suleiman and his successors commissioned hundreds of fabulous public buildings. Best-known are the great mosques of Constantinople. They compliment the ancient, massive dome of Haghia Sophia along the dragon's-back skyline of the city, making modern Istanbul one of the most beautiful cities in the world.

The man who designed most of these buildings is called Sinan the Architect. Born 'Joseph' to Greek Orthodox parents in central Anatolia, he was collected as a tribute youth in 1512 and converted to Islam receiving the name 'Sinan', 'the spearhead'. His father was a stonemason and, perhaps because of this, he ended up in the engineering regiment of the Janissaries where he soon made his mark. He was in charge of mining operations at the siege of Vienna in 1529 and after that he was put in charge of building military bridges and the like. Finally in 1538 he was made *Mimar Bashi*, Chief Architect to the sultan. Sinan was a genius. He borrowed freely from Christian, Byzantine forms. You can see their influence in the domes of his remarkable buildings.

Like most Janissaries, Sinan was a member of the *Bektashi* order of dervishes, part of the liberal, *suffi* form of Islam and therefore appealing to men who'd begun life as Christians. Women could take part in some *Bektashi* rituals and the *Bektashis* were not averse to drinking wine. They were unfanatical. The Grand Vizier Rüstem Pasha, who commissioned work from Sinan in the 1560s, was fairly typical. He believed that Christians, Jews, and even Shiite Muslims, the lowest of the low by orthodox Islamic standards, could all find their way to heaven - insofar as he believed in anything at all.

The Laughing One

But even as these great buildings began to soar skywards, the seeds of decline were germinating in the palace of the sultans. In the hypnotic silence of Topkapi, all was not as it should be. In 1523, Turkish raiders had captured a Russian girl as part of a trawl through Galicia in what is now southern Poland. Called 'Hürrem', the Laughing One, because of her wit, she was pretty rather than beautiful but she had charm and intelligence and she was singled out for the sultan's harem. Within a year she'd given Suleiman a son and had risen to become second Sultana -

third in the harem after the sultan's mother and the mother of his first son.

Suleiman was besotted. The first Sultana was cast aside. Hürrem, or Roxelana as she's better known (possibly meaning 'Russian girl'), became the sole object of his love. She even persuaded him to marry her, the first marriage of a sultan since the humiliation of Beyazit's wife being forced to serve naked at Tamerlane's table back in 1402. To make sure of her position, she suggested that he marry off all the younger, prettier women of the harem, arguing that it wasn't fair to keep them since Suleiman now slept only with her.

In the 1540s, following a fire which destroyed much of the old harem, Roxelana moved into new rooms right next door to Suleiman's apartments and had a private door cut between them. She could now watch proceedings of the Divan, the royal council, through a latticed window, and she began to learn the art of government.

Thus began the rule of the harem, the 'Sultanate of Women' as it's sometimes known. Harem women had always conducted vicious power struggles behind the scenes, but now 'harem intrigues' started to influence policy. It wasn't the fault of the women. Denied a public role, ambitious women had no choice but to realise their ambitions from behind the scenes.

The problem was that the women could only achieve power through their sons. Given that all other potential heirs to the throne were strangled on the accession of each new sultan, this was a life or death matter. Roxelana's main aim was thus to secure the succession of one of her sons, in which she succeeded. However her first victim, if that's the right word, was Suleiman's Grand Vizier, Ibrahim.

Ibrahim, originally a Greek tribute slave, had been Suleiman's boon companion for years. The two men were inseparable, sleeping and eating together. In truth, Ibrahim was the author of his own downfall. He was critical of Roxelana and he became too big for his boots, openly boasting that he could overrule Suleiman whenever he wanted to and that he, Ibrahim, was the real power in the land. All Roxelana had to do was to bring this to Suleiman's attention.

Ibrahim was found strangled at the palace gate one March morning in 1536.

The Kul

Modern Turkey has a democratic feel to it. There is no tradition of aristocracy. No snobbery percolates down from the top.

This is because the Ottoman Empire was run by the sultan's extended, slave household, the *Kul*. The *Kul* was made up of the brightest of the boys drawn from the *devsirme*, the boy-tribute. Most of the high officials, including even the Grand Viziers, were slaves owing no allegiance except to their sultan. The word 'slave' is a rather poor translation of their status. They were 'owned' by their sultan but they couldn't be bought or sold and they could gain huge wealth during their lives.

But when they *did* die, all their wealth reverted to the sultan. Thus no hereditary class could develop. Only the sultanate was hereditary, but the sultan himself was probably the son of a slave on his mother's side and at least half the son of a slave on his father's side. The later Ottoman sultans had very little Turkish blood in their veins at all.

THE SOT AND OTHER BLOTS
THE SLIPPERY SLOPE

In Brief	
1566	Death of Suleiman the Magnificent.
1570	Cyprus taken for Selim the Sot
1571	Battle of Lepanto - Ottoman fleet defeated by Christian Alliance.
1603	Start of the 'Golden Cage' - end of the tradition of fratricide

Stuffed Sultan

By 1566 Suleiman the Magnificent was a tired, old man and a widower (Roxelana died in 1558), but he took his army for one last campaign into Hungary. He besieged the key castle of Szigetvr which held out to the bitter end, only falling after the Turks exploded a gigantic mine beneath the inner fortifications. Suleiman, who was ill with an ulcerous leg and other ailments, stayed in his tent for most of the siege and showed no signs of approval when it was over. On the journey back to Belgrade his soldiers, although laden with booty, were uneasy and Suleiman, travelling with them in a heavily-curtained litter, was oddly uncommunicative.

He'd been dead for six weeks, from three days before the castle fell, from the night when the giant mine had exploded. Only four men were in on the secret, one of them being his doctor and another his Grand Vizier, a remarkable man by the name of Sokollu Mehmet Pasha who'd started out as a Bosnian tribute youth. Fearing for the morale of the army, they'd gutted Suleiman's body and buried the innards beneath the floor of the tent, covering it over with a Persian carpet. Then they'd embalmed the body, redressed it in his royal robes and painted the face so that it looked like he was still alive. Finally, they'd arranged him in his chair so as to stiffen into position. Viewed through a gauze curtain, the effect was quite convincing. They only told the army of the death after Sultan Selim, Suleiman's successor and third son (by Roxelana), had been informed and was on his way to meet them.

The good life
Poor Selim wasn't a patch on Suleiman. He was a short, reddish-bearded man who waddled when he walked and drank too much. The Turks have never been a puritanical lot - Suleiman wasn't averse to the odd glass of wine - but Selim drank wine by the litre from half a double-coconut-shell set in jewelled gold. He set a standard of luxurious living for his like-minded subjects to follow.

During the sixteenth century, the Turkish Empire doubled in population. By the early seventeenth century, Constantinople, by far the largest city in Europe, consumed seven million sheep and lambs and over

200,000 cattle per year along with countless other provisions. It was immensely wealthy.

Mostly, sixteenth-century Turks followed Selim's example and enjoyed the fruits of their success. Constantinople, with its panorama of gardens and broad-eaved houses tumbling down to the Bosphorus, was a good place to live. Suleiman had legalised coffee and the men could sit and chat in the new coffee houses over a hubble-bubble and a cup of their favourite brew, as could the women, although more privately in the *hamams* or bath houses, a central feature of Turkish life.

Although veiled, Turkish women were in some ways freer than their western counterparts. Indoors they laid aside their veils and if a man, on returning home, saw the shoes of a woman visitor at the door, he was unable to enter his own harem. Unlike in the west, women could own property even when married. And who knew what they were up to beneath those veils when they were out and about? Some, according to Lady Mary Wortley Montague, wife of a British ambassador in the eighteenth century, met their lovers without ever exposing their faces, thus protecting themselves against gossip and its consequences.

A big mistake
Despite the pleasant lifestyle, by 1566 when Selim the Sot ascended the throne, the Ottoman Empire was already rotting from within although this wasn't immediately obvious. The rot had started under Suleiman - not only the rule of the Harem but also military failure. In 1537, after an indecisive campaign in the Balkans, he'd become the first sultan to return home without booty, and, of course, he'd failed to take Vienna in 1529. But under Selim the rot progressed more rapidly. Selim's only major military

success was the capture of Cyprus in 1570 by Sokullu Mehmet Pasha, a very bloody affair and undertaken for no better reason than that Selim wanted to secure a supply of his favourite Cypriot wine.

The invasion of Cyprus was a mistake, a big mistake. It shocked the Christian world because it was brutal and utterly uncalled for. The Christian powers responded by forming a 'Holy Alliance' led by Spain, then the western superpower.

The Turks had never fancied themselves as sailors - 'the sea is for Christians', they used to say - but actually they were quite good at it. Under Suleiman's Admiral Barbarossa (died 1546) their black-painted galleys had raided far into the western Mediterranean, over-wintering in Toulon, France, in 1543. Muslim pirates from North Africa (Turks by another name as far as the west was concerned) had raided as far as the coasts of Britain. But it was at sea that the tide finally turned against the Turks.

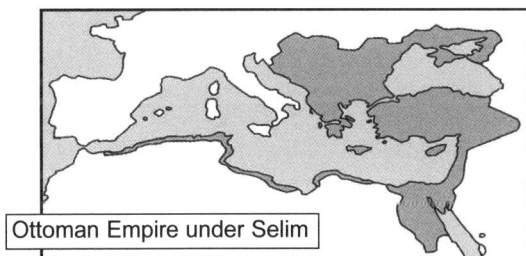

Ottoman Empire under Selim

Lepanto
On Sunday 7 October 1571, the Turkish fleet and the fleet of the Christian Holy Alliance, commanded by Don Jon of Austria, bastard half-brother of Philip II of Spain, met off the Greek shore just out from the small town of Lepanto. The Turks with 273 galleys slightly outnumbered the Christians but the Turkish ships were smaller on average and the Christian ships were better armed with cannon.

For a while the two fleets faced each other in silence across the blue waters, then the watching Christians saw a small puff of white smoke rise from a cannon on the Turkish admiral's flagship. As if on cue, cannon roared, whips cracked and thousands of galley slaves on both sides put their backs to the oars, oars which creaked and groaned as the fleets moved slowly towards each other.

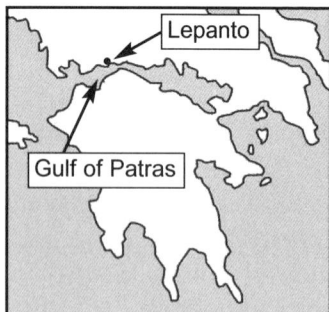

Lepanto was the last great naval battle ever to be fought with galleys. The Turkish flagship rammed the flagship of Don Jon of Austria. The two ships became hopelessly entangled and other ships joined in to help their respective commanders until the centre of the battle had turned into a knotted island of ships where the fighting was mostly hand to hand. 'The sea foamed with blood' as one Christian participant described the scene. The Turkish ships lay lower in the water than the Christian ships and were more easily boarded and, although the Turks fought like lions, as the day wore on one ship after another was lost to the enemy. By evening 20,000 Turks had perished compared to around 8,000 Christians and the Turkish fleet had been comprehensively thrashed.

Strangulation - again

Selim the Sot wasn't present at the Battle of Lepanto. Sultans didn't usually sail with their fleets. But, whether on land or at sea, the days when sultans led their forces in person were almost over. They simply weren't the men they used to be. This was due in large measure to the tradition of fratricide, the strangling of brothers. Fratricide meant that each reigning sultan had no uncles, no great uncles and of course no brothers to challenge him and limit his excesses. If a sultan wanted to lay waste an island in search of wine, who was to stop him? There was only the harem - and the Janissaries, but more of them later.

On 10 December 1574, Selim, who was probably drunk, slipped and cracked his head while examining a new bathhouse in Topkapi, designed by Sinan the Architect. Sinan, then aged eighty-five, had gone ahead to open the door to the hot room and was unable to move back fast enough to help. Selim himself had avoided the need for fratricide when he came to the throne back in 1566 because both his brothers were already dead, but on Selim's death, his son Murad III (1574-95) ordered the strangulation of *five* younger brothers. And when Murad died in 1595, his son, Mehmet III (1595-1603), had *nineteen* brothers and all his sisters strangled. The oldest brother was just eleven.

The Cage

After the appalling Mehmet III, came Mehmet's son, Ahmet I (1603-17). Ahmet was made of kinder stuff. He cast around for a humane alternative to brother-killing and came up with the 'Golden Cage'. From 1603 onwards, all royal princes were locked up in the *kafes* or Cage, a grey, two-storied building hidden in the depths of the harem. From now on, the succession went to the eldest son to avoid 'arguments' and not to the ablest as had been the custom before. In the Golden Cage the princes lived lives of insufferable boredom with only the company of specially sterilised concubines to entertain them. When each new sultan emerged blinking into the light of day, he was a weird shell of a man with little understanding of the outside world.

The Cage produced inadequates and monsters. Monsters like Ibrahim (1640-48). Ibrahim was shut in the cage at the age of two and only emerged at twenty-four when he became sultan. By then he was mad. He became obsessed by fur, specifically sable. His clothing was festooned with sable, the walls of his rooms were lined with it from floor to ceiling and his cats wore jackets made out of it. Towards the end of his reign he drowned all his two hundred and eighty concubines (bar one and his favourite, a large, fat Armenian known as 'Sugar-Bit') by having them tied in sacks and dropped into the Sea of Marmara. A diver sent to inspect a shipwreck reported:

Many sacks, each holding the body of a woman, standing upright at the weighted end and swaying in the current.

Behind palace walls

Ibrahim's atrocity notwithstanding, the population of women in the harem spiralled out of control. By the 1680s, the number of inmates was over four thousand, a major drain on finances since they were all slaves, they cost a fortune to buy and each of them required expensive clothing. When they were freed to marry elsewhere, which was quite normal, they took their expensive clothes and jewels with them. In this claustrophobic, perfumed world, real power lay with the sultan's mother and one or two other senior women, and with the Chief Black Eunuch. ('Black' because he was from Africa.) Eunuchs were the only men allowed in the harem, apart from the sultan and the sultan's sons.

The world of the later sultans was very weird. Edward Barton, ambassador for Queen Elizabeth I of England, described his formal introduction. He was first dressed in a special gold robe and then had to wait outside the 'Gate of Felicity', the entrance to the inner court, among a bunch of eunuchs, deaf mutes, dwarfs and other 'courtiers'. On entering the royal presence, his arms were seized and pinned to his sides (a precaution against assassination) and he was frog-marched towards the throne to kiss the royal hand. His presents were presented and, at the end of this bizarre experience, he was dragged backwards out of the room. The sultan scarcely uttered a word.

Small wonder that the Ottoman government became known in Europe as the 'Sublime Porte' (from the French *porte* meaning door). This was the name given to the gateway to the Grand Vizier's mansion where ambassadors left their credentials when they first arrived in Constantinople. It was the Grand Vizier who conducted most of the business of government - leaving his master to other amusements.

If you're in Istanbul
The Sublime Porte is a monumental gate situated at the corner of Alemdar Caddesi and Alayköskü, on the road which winds up from the Golden Horn towards Sultanahmet and Haghia Sophia. It was once the entrance to a complex of government buildings.

HE WORE A GIANT SPOON
COOKING POTS AND A NASTY SPAT

In Brief	
1648	Janissaries replace Ibrahim with Mehmet IV.
1683	Second siege of Vienna
1808	Mahmud the Reformer becomes Sultan.
1826	The Auspicious Event - the supression of the Janissaries.

Janissaries

In 1648, shortly after the drowning of Ibrahim's concubines, the Grand Mufti, top spiritual expert of the Muslims, called a meeting in the central mosque of Haghia Sophia. He demanded that Ibrahim be overthrown. Only one anonymous voice in all the huge crowd spoke out against his proposal and that voice received no backing.

The Grand Mufti had prepared his ground well. Even Ibrahim's mother agreed that her mad son must go. More importantly - so did the Janissaries. After the meeting at Haghia Sophia, the Janissaries marched to the Palace and forced Ibrahim to return to the Golden Cage, there to be strangled by deaf mutes a few days later.

The Janissaries had become very powerful. They still called the reigning sultan their 'Little Father', but their loyalty was now only skin-deep. In 1638, Ibrahim's predecessor, Sultan Murad IV, had abolished the *devshirme*, the boy tribute, and from then on the Janissary ranks had been replenished with the sons of former Janissaries rather than by hand-picked slave youths. They became arrogant. They strutted round Constantinople, armed to the teeth and in swanky turbans, dishing out justice as and when they saw fit. A large tree, the 'Janissary Tree', grew at the centre of the Hippodrome. This was where they held their meetings and where they called for the overturning of cooking pots as a signal for mutiny. From its branches they hung the bodies of their victims.

Leisure time - for some

In spite of the Janissaries, seventeenth-century Turkey was still an amazing place to live. Constantinople, the capital of an international empire, was very cosmopolitan. In its crowded streets, Albanians in baggy pantaloons made deals with Egyptians in long dish-dashes, Jews from Iraq took coffee with Greeks from Athens, westerners in stuffy wigs and waistcoats shouldered past weathered tribesmen from Central Asia, and there were Turks everywhere of course. All colours and creeds (bar some Muslim sects) were welcome in the Empire although the authorities insisted on certain distinctions among the non-Muslims if they were resident: Greeks had to wear black shoes, Armenians had to wear crimson shoes and Jews had to wear pale blue shoes.

Out in the countryside, conditions were harsh but, in the large cities, life for most middling Turkish families was still very pleasant and for the rich it was very pleasant indeed. Most households could afford a domestic slave or two and some had lots of them. In public, these slaves were painfully obsequious to their masters or mistresses but, just as women laid aside their veils in the privacy of the home, so slaves tended to lay aside their servility once they stepped indoors. They were often remarkably informal with their masters and mistresses. The Turkish concept of slavery wasn't an absolute - after seven years servitude many slaves were given their freedom. Indeed, among pious Muslims it was a virtuous act to free a slave, and children fathered by owners on slave girls could inherit along with the children of legitimate wives.

Dinner time

The seventeenth century was when Turkish cooking became one of the great cuisines of the world. Small wonder since they had an empire of flavours to choose from: dates from Egypt, sultanas from North Africa, olives from the Mediterranean shore and countless other fruits, meats, cereals and vegetables. The improvement of recipes was driven by the palace where over 1,300 kitchen staff laboured to please the royal taste-buds as well as an army of hungry concubines, wives and eunuchs and huge numbers of guests and hangers-on. Sublime pastries both sweet and savoury, delicate rice dishes, pancakes, sweets, a multitude of different styles of bread, all were brought to a new peak of tasty excellence. Some dishes, especially the sweets, were produced (and still are) by skilled craftsmen belonging to specialist guilds.

Legend has it that *Lokum* or 'Turkish Delight' was first developed in this period on the orders of a sultan who demanded a new and perfect sweetmeat and that it was evolved after much research in the palace kitchens. Actually it has its roots in Anatolia and goes at least as far back as the fifteenth century. The old recipes included honey, grape molasses and flour but in the seventeenth century, refined cane sugar became available and the research in the palace may have come about as a result of the availability of sugar. Whatever its origins, Turkish Delight later became highly fashionable as a gift, especially between courting couples. It came wrapped in special lace handkerchiefs.

Recipe for Turkish Delight

What you will need

2 tablespoons lemon juice	rind of 1 medium lemon
2 tablespoons gelatine	rind of 1 medium orange
3 cups caster sugar	1/4 cup (2 fl oz) orange juice
1/2 cup (4 oz) water	3-4 drops rose water
1 cup (8 fl oz) water	1/2 cup icing sugar
2/3 cup cornflour	Oil or butter

1.Line a deep 17 cm square cake tin with aluminum foil, leaving edges hanging over, then brush foil with oil or melted butter.

2. Remove white pith from rinds of the orange and lemon, then mix the juices and the rinds, the sugar and water in large pan.

3. Stir over a medium heat until sugar has dissolved, but without boiling.

4. Remove any sugar crystals from the sides of pan with a wet pastry brush.

5. Bring to boil, then reduce heat slightly and boil without stirring until a teaspoon of mixture dropped into cold water forms long threads.

69

6. Mix gelatine with 1/2 cup (4 fl oz) extra water in mixing bowl. Stir over hot water (to keep it warm) until the gelatine is dissolved.

7. In separate bowl combine cornflour with small quantity of water and mix until smooth.

8. Add the gelatine and cornflour mixtures to the sugar syrup. Stir over medium heat until the mixture boils and clears.

9. Mix in the rose water.

10. Strain mixture into cake tin and place in the fridge; refrigerate overnight.

11. When it has set, peel off the foil and cut into squares. Roll in icing sugar.

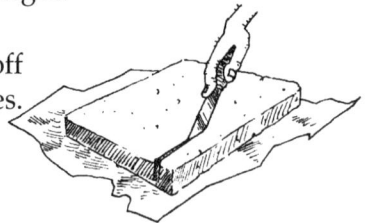

Vienna (again)

While affluent Turks lived lives of plenty, the war machine continued to function, setting out each spring for the borders. But the machine was getting rusty. To reinvigorate things, in 1683 the decision was taken to have another try at Vienna. A vast army of 200,000 regulars trudged or trotted north, beefed up by 15,000 Turkoman irregulars from the steppes of Asia, men so fierce that even the Turks were frightened of them. By July, the citizens of Vienna were under siege for the second time, their 11,000 defenders again vastly outnumbered. By 4 September, food had almost run out and the Viennese were down to eating donkeys.

That day, 4 September 1683, Vienna was rocked by a gigantic and sudden explosion. It tore a huge hole in the inner wall of the city. The Turks had tunnelled beneath and packed their tunnel with explosives.

The city was now practically defenceless. The Turks could easily have finished the job, but for some reason Kara Mustafa, the Grand Vizier, failed to press home his attack. Fighting desperately, the Viennese held off a series of limited assaults over the next few days, and meanwhile a German relief force marched to the rescue. While the Turks continued to concentrate on the city, the Germans took up position on a series of ridges surrounding the enormous but unprotected Turkish camp. Next morning they attacked in force. The result was inevitable. In spite of fighting ferociously, the Turks were comprehensively trounced. Legend has it that the bakers of Vienna celebrated their miraculous escape by inventing the croissant, in the shape of the Islamic crescent moon*. The oddly incompetent Kara Mustafa led the remains of his tattered army south and the order for his head arrived shortly after. It was delivered to Sultan Mehmet IV in the traditional velvet bag.

Downhill slide

The failed second siege of Vienna was a turning point. From the mid-seventeenth century, Turkey experienced a

*This legend is also applied to the siege of Belgrade in 1686. The definitive origin of the croissant has not yet been established.

string of almost continuous defeats and setbacks stretching into the twentieth century. The first three were shattering:

1664: defeat by the Austrians at St. Gotthard.
1683: failure of Second Siege of Vienna.
1699: Peace of Karlowitz, territory lost to European powers.

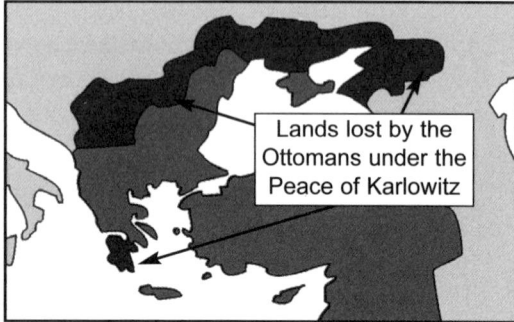

Lands lost by the Ottomans under the Peace of Karlowitz

Europe leapt ahead and the Ottoman Empire trailed behind. There were some footling efforts to catch up. In the 1720s, the first Ottoman ambassadors arrived in the west and, at about the same time, the first printing presses were set up in Constantinople. But nothing much came of these moves. Few people saw the need. Nothing could shake an invincible sense of superiority however unwarranted in the circumstances.

Rampant corruption, arrogant Janissaries, a creaking government machine - the sultans simply weren't up to the job of putting things right. It was utterly inconceivable to them that their giant Empire could fade away and so they went right on enjoying themselves despite all the signs of political decay. They buried their heads in the cushions of their harems. Pleasure and a life of ease were their priorities and unfortunately this set the tone for many of their top officials as well.

Tulip time

The Tulip Craze (tulips grow wild in Anatolia) was typical. The first signs of tulip-mania had appeared back in the reign of Suleiman the Magnificent (1520-66) and from there the craze had spread to Holland in the seventeenth century. But in the 1720s, under Sultan Ahmed III (1703-30), it returned to Turkey with a vengeance. Tulips became so popular that a single bulb might cost more than a horse. Each April for several years, Sultan Ahmed held a tulip festival in the palace. Thousands of tulips were displayed by night on miles of special shelving,preferably under a full moon. Between the vases were bowls of coloured water which distributed the light from myriad lamps of coloured glass. From the branches of the trees, hung cages of twittering canaries.

It looked very pretty and it cost a fortune, but it had nothing to do with modernisation. In 1779, Russia took the Crimea.

French Sultana

European influences were increasing. Sometime in the early 1780s, a French ship *en route* from France to Martinique was captured by Algerian pirates. On board was a gorgeous young girl by the name of Aimée Dubucq de Rivery, travelling back to Martinique from her convent school in France. Aimée had golden hair, blue eyes and a pert nose. She was so gorgeous that the Bey (commander) of Algiers decided to offer her as a present to Sultan Abdul

Hamid I (reigned 1774-89). Abdul Hamid, then aged fifty-nine, was overjoyed and promptly fell in love with his gift.

Aimée must have been very adaptable, although after the restrictions of convent life the royal harem may not have seemed so dreadful. There are worse things than lolling around draped in precious stones while slave girls massage your feet and bring you tasty nibbles on exquisite golden trays. Aimée walked the 'Golden Road' (a long corridor) to the sultan's bedroom without complaint as far as we know and before long she gave Abdul Hamid a son. She had secured her position in the harem.

If you're in Istanbul
The Golden Road is a long corridor that runs down the side of the Topkapi harem, on the side of the second court of the Palace. It's rather a gloomy corridor.

Abdul Hamid was no monster and Aimée was fond of him. He allowed his heir and nephew, Selim, considerable freedom. Selim became friendly with Aimée and she read to him, suitably veiled no doubt - in French.

When Abdul Hamid died in 1789, three months before the start of the French Revolution, Selim took over as sultan. Seven years later, by an extraordinary coincidence, a cousin and childhood friend of Aimée's by the name of Josephine Beauharnais married Napoleon Bonaparte, the new leader of France, and became the Empress Josephine. Now the two beautiful cousins from Martinique were connected to two of the most powerful men in the world.

Because of Aimée, Sultan Selim III (reigned 1789-1807) was a fan of most things French and longed to reform his empire using ideas from the west. He started a newspaper, *Le Moniteur de l'Orient*, formed a 'New Army', based on

French principles and designed to be a counterweight to the Janissaries, and he employed French officers to train the Turkish navy. Given Selim's pro-French attitude and the friendship between Aimée and Empress Josephine, Turkey and France should have been natural allies but in 1798 at the height of the Napoleonic War, Napoleon invaded the Turkish province of Egypt and, to add insult to injury, he did it to get at the British - to cut the quickest route to British interests in India.

In spite of Selim's best endeavours, the Turks scarcely mattered any more.

Deaf mutes, black eunuchs - and an act of mercy
Poor Selim, he reformed things when he dared but he had to tread very carefully. In 1807 he got it badly wrong. He ordered some of the younger, fitter Janissaries to join his New Army and the Janissaries mutinied. They rampaged through Constantinople in protest. The heads of New Army officers were stuck on poles and paraded before the palace walls. To avoid further bloodshed, Selim handed the throne to his half-mad half-brother and heir, Mustafa IV (1807-08), and retired in dignified fashion to the Golden Cage.

At this point, one of Selim's generals, a loyal soldier by the name of Alemdar Mustafa, marched to his rescue with 40,000 troops, arriving on 28 July 1808. Alemdar left his main army outside the city and made his way to the palace accompanied by a troop of picked men.

With Alemdar hammering on the palace gate, Mustafa's only chance was now to execute both Selim and the next in line to the throne, Aimée's son Mahmud, so that he, Mustafa, would be the only Ottoman left and therefore irreplaceable. He unleashed the deaf mutes. There was a desperate struggle in Selim's mother's apartment. Selim managed to stab two of his attackers before being killed by the chief Black Eunuch, and he had time to send warning to Aimée. The deaf mutes sprinted down the Golden Road towards Mahmud but they were held up when a beefy female slave threw hot coals at them. Mahmud climbed through a chimney with seconds to spare and hid under some old clothes, lying motionless while the deaf mutes searched a neighbouring room.

Alemdar, the loyal general, had meanwhile forced his way into the palace. He caught Mustafa in the throne room and was about to cut him down when young Mahmud made a dramatic reappearance covered in soot.

Mahmud II the Reformer's first act as sultan was to stay Alemdar's hand and to grant mercy to Mustafa who was sent to the Cage.

The Auspicious Event
Once again the Janissaries had proved their power even if they'd been outmanoeuvred by General Alemdar. Secretly Mahmud swore vengeance, but he had to wait eighteen years to get it.

He laid his plans carefully and well in advance. Meanwhile, the Janissaries grew more obnoxious. At Easter, they spread their cloaks on the ground and made Christians pay to walk across them, they opened shops in competition with other traders then cheated on their suppliers and customers, they extorted protection money and they sang obscene songs on Fridays, the Muslim Holy Day. Finally, in June 1826, reckoning that he'd given the Janissaries enough rope to hang themselves, Mahmud pounced. He decreed that they be incorporated into the New Army, knowing full well that this would provoke them to mutiny.

Mutiny they did, a month later. The traditional cauldrons were lugged out of the barracks and overturned and they all made for the Atmaidan, the open space where the Hippodrome had once stood. Mahmud sent four officers to parley with them and they killed the officers on the spot and marched on the palace. This was the moment Mahmud had been waiting for. He'd assembled a force of 14,000 artillerymen and with this force behind him he now appeared before the Janissaries, on a white horse and with the black standard of the Prophet Mohammed, and imperiously demanded their obedience. When the Janissaries responded insolently, two cannon fired grapeshot and cut a bloody swathe through their ranks. Shocked, the Janissaries fled back towards the Atmaidan but there more cannon awaited them. They fled to their barracks and locked themselves in. Kara Djehennem, 'Black Hell', the artillery commander, brought his cannon up to the barracks gates so that no one could leave, then he set fire to the barracks while pounding them with volley after volley.

Over 10,000 men died that day and in subsequent mopping-up operations. On Friday 16 June 1826, a *firman* (royal decree) abolished the Janissaries for ever.

The destruction of the Janissaries has gone down in Turkish history as the 'Auspicious Event'. From now on, Mahmud was able to speed up his reforms. He opened schools and continued to reform the armed services. In 1829 he decreed that his all subjects, except the mullahs, give up their turbans and baggy pantaloons. From now on, men had to wear tight black trousers, a frock coat and a fez.

It was the end of an era.

If you're in Istanbul

The ancient Hippodrome, where the Byzantines conducted their chariot races, renamed the Atmaidan, was the heart of Ottoman Constantinople for four hundred years after the Turkish conquest. It runs from beside the Blue Mosque towards Haghia Sophia and it remains a public open space.

TOO MUCH SEX
OR NOT ENOUGH?

In Brief	
1827	Battle of Navarino.
1830	Greek Independence.
1853-56	Crimean War
1865	Society of New Ottomans formed.
1876-78	National Assembly.
1877	Russian invasion.
1906	Committee of Union and Progress formed - start of the Young Turks.

Shopping

Mahmud the Reformer, in spite of his many virtues including the destruction of the Janissaries, was rather too fond of champagne, with gilt-covered opium pills afterwards to ease the hangovers. His drunkenness upset his favourite wife, a former bathroom attendant by the name of Besma, so Besma steered their son, Abdul Mejid, away from the bottle and towards the pleasures of the harem instead. Abdul responded with enthusiasm and from a remarkably young age considering the nature of the activity required of him. The result, so it is said, was that he became impotent - and took to the bottle.

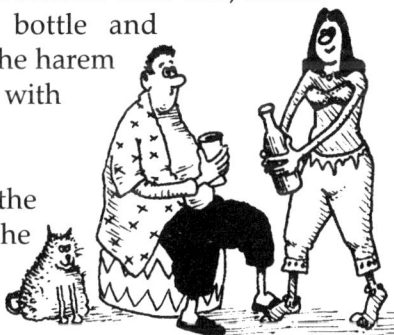

Perhaps to compensate for his growing impotence, from

79

the moment he came to the throne at the age of sixteen, Sultan Abdul Mejid (1839-61) was always wildly extravagant. Starting in 1839, he set about building the Dolmabaçe Palace, a grandiose folly covering half a mile of reclaimed land along the Bosphorus to the west of the Golden Horn. The Dolmabaçe had (and still has) 285 rooms, the largest mirrors in the world, a four-ton chandelier in the ballroom and fourteen tons of gold leaf were used in its construction. To add to the spending, in a misguided nod towards liberalism Abdul Mejid allowed members of his harem to go into shops when they went shopping, rather than wait outside in their carriages. Seeing so much on offer, the veiled beauties shopped till they dropped. Besma, although perhaps no longer a beauty, was one of the worst offenders.

If you're in Istanbul

Dolmabaçe means 'filled-up garden'. The Dolmabaçe Palace occupies a superb site beside the Bosphorus. It was built on land reclaimed from the water in the time of Suleiman the Magnificent. Sixteen thousand Christian slaves were employed on the project.

The Greek rebellion

Abdul Mejid's grasp on reality was faint. While he built palaces and ordered shopping expeditions, Turkey fell further into disrepair. In January 1824, a slightly portly former heart-throb and celebrity poet by the name of George Gordon, Lord Byron, had stepped ashore at the Greek port of Mesolongi in a brand-new scarlet uniform, bringing with him a ship full of arms and a chest full of money for Greek rebels against Ottoman rule. Byron was classically educated and his love of the ancient Greeks had given him a rosy picture of their less-than-classical descendants. His arrival gave a huge boost to the Greek rebellion.

The Greek rebellion was decidedly bloody. It began in 1821, three years before Byron's arrival (and untimely death), when the Greeks massacred every Muslim they could lay their hands on, women and children included. The uprising was subdued, with equal nastiness, by a Muslim army (1825-26) but then the Turkish fleet was annihilated by the British, at the Battle of Navarino off the Greek coast (1827), and the Muslim army was cut off and forced to withdraw. Thanks to British intervention, Greece became independent in 1830.

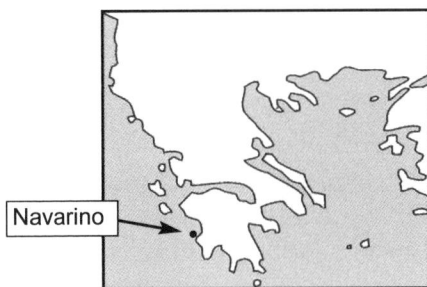

Sick man of Europe
The Muslim army that subdued the rebels in 1825 came from Egypt and was led by Ibrahim Pasha son of the semi-independent governor of Egypt, a ruthless man by the name of Mehmet Pasha. Ibrahim Pasha was defeated by a combined British, French and Russian naval force - Turkey had almost nothing to do with it.

Turkey had become the 'Sick Man of Europe', a helpless invalid squabbled over by greedy western powers. But what each western power wanted was to make sure that none of the others got their hands on the corpse when the invalid finally keeled over and died, so none of them gained very much at all.

Things came to a head in 1853, in the Crimean War, when the British and the French, with some help from the Turks, stopped the Russians from invading Turkey from the north. Back in the capital, many Turks were so behind the times that they were less concerned about the possibility of a Russian victory than they were at the thought, shock-horror, of Florence Nightingale tending male soldiers at Scutari, modern Üsküdar, just across the Bosphorus.

Time please

In Europe people were building steam trains; in Turkey life went on at its old, slow pace. Abdul Mejid spent money like water. He built another palace, the Küçüksu Kasri, and a lot of clock towers in towns around Anatolia and Thrace. The clock towers should have been a sign of progress but, like the shopping, they somehow missed the point. Turkish time was stubbornly different to western time. The day began at sunrise but since sunrise changes throughout the year, the clocks had to be adjusted to fit. Nobody could ever be completely sure what hour it was and people were always fiddling with their watches.

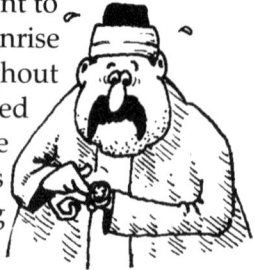

If you're in Istanbul

There's a very fine, elaborate clock tower built by Sultan Abdul Hamid II (1876-1909) right by the tourist entrance to the Dolmabaçe Palace by the Bosphorus. Inside the Palace, all the clocks read 9.05 am, the exact time when Ataturk died, in a room upstairs, overlooking the Bosphorus, on 10th November 1938.

When he died in 1861, Abdul Mejid was massively in debt to western banks. The next sultan, his brother Abdul Aziz (1861-76), was just as profligate. Abdul Aziz was a large man with very large appetites. He acquired a harem of nine hundred concubines and built yet another palace, the Beylerbeyi, on the Asian side of the Bosphorus. Debt soared and soared.

Finally, in 1875, Abdul Aziz refused to pay interest on his debts.

The Turkish Empire had effectively declared itself bankrupt.

> **If you're in Istanbul**
> The small(ish) Beylerbeyi Palace on the Asian shore of the Bosphorus is well worth a visit. Sultan Abdul Hamid II, deposed by the Young Turks in 1909, lived his last years there (1913-18). He was a keen cabinetmaker and much of the furniture in the Palace was made by him.

New Ottomans

Not all Turks worried about what foreign nurses might be up to or what time it was, and relatively few of them could afford to go shopping. By the 1860s, a growing band of the educated wanted to put right what was wrong with their country. In 1865, the 'Society of New Ottomans' was formed and held its first meeting in Constantinople with 245 founder members.

The aim was reform without revolution: they were moderate Muslims. But reform had to start at the top. As things stood, there was nothing to stop the reigning sultan spending the entire wealth of the state on toothpaste if he so desired. What was needed, according to the New Ottomans, was a constitutional monarchy somewhat along the lines of Britain.

Abdul Aziz tried to suppress the New Ottomans but, whatever he did to them individually, their ideas wouldn't go away and they had supporters in the government. Meanwhile he went quietly mad. The symptoms were bizarre: for fear of poison, he lived for days on nothing but hard-boiled eggs, he refused to read government documents written in black ink, he ordered all government officials called Aziz to change their names - and he chased poultry around the vast halls of Dolmabaçe laughing like a jackass. If he caught one, he decorated it with medals for gallantry. What's more, the bird had to wear its medals afterwards.

This was no way to run a chicken coop let alone an empire. Something had to give. In April 1876, the Bulgarians rebelled and were savagely repressed. News of the repression reached western Europe causing widespread revulsion - and the possible threat of intervention.

The Grand Vizier at that time was a remarkable man called Midhat Pasa, a sympathiser with the New Ottomans. Abdul Aziz had appointed him to appease growing opposition to his rule although he hated Midhat for having once worn spectacles in the royal presence. Reluctantly Midhat decided to engineer a coup. On 29 May 1876, he and the foreign minister entered the palace backed up by troops. Abdul Aziz was woken from his eight-foot-long, solid-silver bed where he lay with his favourite concubine. After a short, unpleasant scene he was put on a boat and taken to the far side of the Bosphorus where he died five days later*. His nephew, Sultan, Murad IV 'the Reformer', was put on the throne instead.

A dream
Unfortunately Murad was 'the Reformer' only because that's what Midhat Pasa called him. In reality he was incapable of reforming anything, least of all himself. He was as deranged as his uncle and an alcoholic to boot (he was addicted to champagne laced with brandy). Up to that moment, he'd lived his entire life hidden away and in fear of assassination. He had to be dragged whimpering to the throne. He was a mistake.

Three months after he became sultan, Murad IV was officially declared insane and released from his obligations.

Although by this stage the Balkans as well as Bulgaria were in a state of rebellion, now at last, there was a breath of hope in the air. The new Sultan, Abdul Hamid II (1876-1909), declared a new constitution. A new National Assembly was to be 'elected by universal suffrage without distinction of race or religion throughout the Ottoman Empire'.

Reformers were elated. Their dream was about to come true.

*Officially, he cut his wrists with a pair of scissors but possibly it was murder.

But that's all it was - a dream. Abdul Hamid granted the constitution in order to get rid of the threat of European intervention and for no other reason. Within weeks, Midhat was dismissed without a thank-you. The National Assembly met but achieved nothing. It was dissolved in 1878.

Yildiz

As things turned out, mean-faced Abdul Hamid II, the last sultan to wield absolute power, was as incompetent as his predecessors and a lot nastier than most of them.

Abdul Hamid's one over-riding emotion was fear: fear of assassins, fear of plots, fear of poisons. Maybe this was rational for an Ottoman sultan but it was disastrous for the country. First of all, he moved the royal establishment to a new palace on high ground above the Bosphorus. Actually, Yildiz was less a palace than a giant maze. Hundreds of separate buildings were set in parkland and connected by corridors and secret tunnels. There was no discernable unifying design. Separate teams of builders and architects worked on different parts so that no one individual had any conception of the overall picture apart from Abdul Hamid himself.

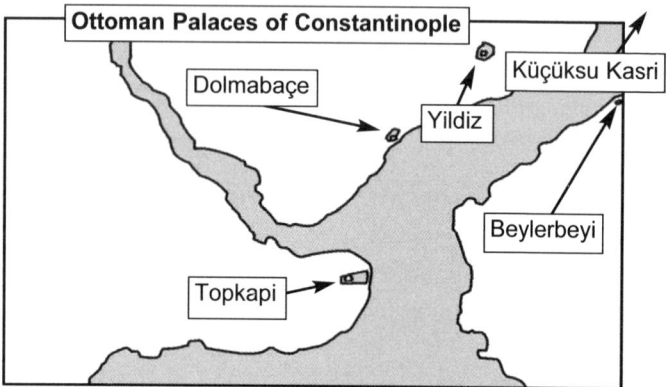

Ottoman Palaces of Constantinople

Dolmabaçe

Küçüksu Kasri

Yildiz

Beylerbeyi

Topkapi

If you're in Istanbul
The Yildiz Palace, high above the Bosphorus between Ortakoy and Besiktas, offers a green retreat from crowded city streets. There's a terrace café at the Malta Kiosk with superb views over the water. It was in the Malta Kiosk that the deposed Murad V lived out his days as a captive of Abdul Hamid II.

It was paranoid heaven. Hundreds of caged parrots were hung among the bushes in the belief that their squawking would sound the alarm on intruders. A prison was placed near to the private zoo so that the screams of those suspected of wanting to harm their sultan would mingle with the shrieks and calls of the animals. No one was allowed to put their hands in their pockets in Abdul Hamid's presence in case they had a weapon but Abdul Hamid himself was always equipped with a gun. (He shot at least two people by accident.) There were guns everywhere. A pair of revolvers hung beside the royal bath.

Here, in the depths of the harem, surrounded by the by now very dated crowd of concubines, deaf mutes and black eunuchs, Abdul Hamid ran things like a spider at the centre of its web. An army of spies, the only government employees guaranteed to receive their salaries, squeezed the last vestiges of hope from his benighted subjects. He himself wasn't above using modern technology when it suited him. Yildiz had electricity when it was forbidden in Constantinople. He used the telegraph to control his officials and his security system.

The end - almost

The problem for the rest of the world was that, in spite of mad sultans, rebellions, massacres, financial chaos and all the other evidence of irreversible decline, the 'Sick Man of Europe' stubbornly refused to die. In 1877 the Russians invaded yet again, using the Bulgarian atrocities as an excuse. Two massive Russian armies marched south into Ottoman territory, a western one into Bulgaria and the other through the Caucasus. Surely this must be the end.

But no. That year Turkey experienced a miracle, the first bit of good news for years. From 20 June to 10 December 1877, the sleepy little town of Plevna (modern Pleven) in Bulgaria was heroically defended by a Turkish force against the much larger, western Russian army. The Turks held out for 143 days against repeated massive assaults.

The defenders were overwhelmed during a magnificent but doomed breakout, but Plevna had bought precious time and given a badly-needed boost to Turkish pride. The Russians reached as far as Adrianople (Edirne), only sixty miles from Constantinople - but they didn't take Constantinople itself.

The Treaty of Berlin which followed (1878) confirmed the independence of Romania, Serbia, Montenegro and part of Bulgaria, and Russia took north-east Anatolia. But at least Turkey was still there.

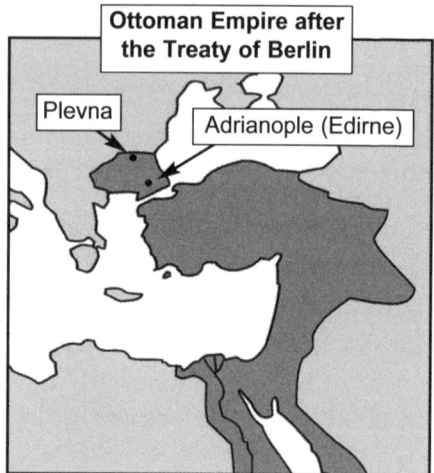

Ottoman Empire after the Treaty of Berlin

Plevna

Adrianople (Edirne)

The end

With every year that passed, the western tide flowed stronger. In 1882, Britain got its hands on Egypt. In 1883, the Orient Express opened for business and, by 1909, wealthy westerners could travel from Paris to Constantinople direct and in luxury to view those quaint, declining Ottomans for themselves. Abdul Hamid twisted and turned, desperate to keep what little power and influence he had left. He played the Muslim card and emphasised that he was still Caliph and therefore leader of all Muslims everywhere. And he played the racist card.

The Christian Armenians have roots in eastern Anatolia and the Caucasus that go back to ancient times. In the 1890s, they were a successful and hard working minority within the Ottoman Empire, and they were quite well liked by the majority, who sometimes referred to them as 'baptised Turks' because they were culturally very similar to the Muslim majority. Abdul Hamid took against them when, egged on by expatriate Armenians in America and elsewhere, they began to demand greater rights and freedoms along with other minorities within his creaking domain. To start with, he banned the word 'Armenian' from school text books and from newspapers but of course the Armenians still existed in reality. He proceeded to harassment and then to cold-blooded murder. Every last detail of the massacres which followed (1894-95) was supervised by Abdul Hamid himself. As in all countries at all times, there were plenty of people willing to respond to hate-filled propaganda. Muslims were given permission to help themselves to the possessions of their Armenian neighbours - and to kill them if they resisted.

It was callous, calculated genocide. Somewhere between 100,000 and 300,000 Armenians lost their lives.

In a sense, the Armenian massacres were the last nail in the Ottoman coffin, and it was Abdul Hamid himself who hammered it in. Decent Turks were appalled by the massacres and by his tyranny. He acquired the nickname 'Abdul the Damned'. At the forefront of his critics were a new, radical group of reformers who had taken the place of the New Ottomans. This new group was known as the 'Young Turks'. The Young Turks had to conduct operations from exile for fear of Abdul Hamid's spies and torture chambers but every day they gained more support - including in the army where many young, German-trained officers became very critical of the government.

In 1906, the 'Committeee of Union and Progress', as the Young Turks now called themselves, established a base in Salonika, over the Bulgarian border in Thessaly. From there they could make their preparations more easily.

WAR!
THE LAST OF THE SULTANS

In Brief

1909	Abdul Hamid forced to abdicate by the Young Turks.
1914	Turkey joins World War I on the side of Germany.
1919	Greeks invade mainland Turkey.
1920	Grand National Assembly established in Ankara.
1921	Battle of Sakkaria - Greeks defeated.
1923	Agreement on population exchange.

Young Turks take power

The Young Turks struck on 2 July 1908. Their call for mutiny spread rapidly through the Turkish army and Sultan Abdul Hamid soon found himself isolated. To avoid open defeat, he caved in to their demands and agreed to reinstate the democratic constitution of 1876. Once again a new National Assembly was to be 'elected by universal suffrage without distinction of race or religion throughout the Ottoman Empire'.

Within a year things had started to go wrong. There was a counter-revolution in Constantinople. Abdul Hamid did nothing to support it openly but he was its figurehead nonetheless. Enver Bey (or Enver Pasha), hero of 1908 and one of the leaders of the Young Turks, marched from Salonika to regain control for the National Assembly.

A room at Yildiz

On 27 April 1909, Enver Bey's troops surrounded the

Palace of Yildiz while a four-man delegation from the National Assembly waited nervously for Abdul Hamid in a room next to the harem. The delegation was watched with almost equal nervousness by thirty eunuchs. The delegation had reason to be nervous. It's not every day that a person is called on to tell an Ottoman sultan that he has to go, and particularly not such a vicious tyrant as Abdul Hamid.

The room was lined with mirrors, each one strategically placed to allow Abdul Hamid advance warning of assassination attempts. A bottle of medicine stood on a table and there was a pile of cigarette butts beside the piano, but as yet there was no sign of Abdul Hamid himself. The delegation continued to wait. When he finally stepped into the room, he was smaller than they'd been expecting and he was wearing an overcoat because the electricity had gone off and there was no heating. He looked thin.

The delegation duly explained their mission. To their considerable relief, Abdul Hamid took the news calmly - once they'd assured him that he wasn't about to be killed. Possibly the news came as a bit of a relief.

That night at midnight, Sultan Abdul Hamid, last absolute monarch of the Ottoman Empire, was put on board his royal train along with three wives, four concubines, four eunuchs, two sons and some servants and sent into exile in Salonika. He was replaced by his brother, Mehmet V, who would reign as constitutional monarch without any real power.

A blot on the landscape

Abdul Hamid's departure sealed the triumph of the Young Turks but Turkey's troubles were far from over. Turkey was weak and predators still waited to take advantage. In 1911 the Bulgarians, Serbs, Montenegrins and Greeks attacked in the Balkans. Edirne in Thrace was only saved at the last minute after a lightning campaign by Enver Bey.

Enver was a very brave soldier. Like the other Young Turks his early dreams were of an empire where all ethnic groups were free and equal. But after his triumph at Edirne he became disillusioned. This was because several major, non-Turkish groups rejected the dream in favour of their individual, ethnic identities. By 1914 his disillusion had become poisonous. That year, when Turkey joined World War I on the side of the Germans, he conceived an obsessive hatred for the Armenians, whom he saw as fifth columnists for the other side. He initiated a second campaign of genocide against them. Once again, there were sufficient people ready to follow a racist lead. The second campaign against the Armenians was even worse than the first. This is no place to go into the horrific details. Suffice it to say that around 600,000 men, women and children were killed.

Mustafa Kemal

One relatively junior Turkish general stood out from the rest during this difficult period - Mustafa Kemal. (Mustafa was the name given to him by his parents, Kemal, meaning 'Perfection', was a nickname given to him at school because he was so good at maths.) Mustafa Kemal was a genius, the man who almost single-handedly created modern Turkey.

At this time he was a rather embittered career officer. He

took no part in the Armenian massacres, he distrusted the Germans and he loathed Enver Bey, now the War Minister and therefore his boss. The two men were complete opposites. Genocidal tendencies aside, Enver was smartly dressed and charming; Mustafa was gruff, difficult, a drinker, a gambler and a womaniser. He's famous for remarking that the quality he found most attractive in a woman was 'availability'.

When things got rough, Mustafa Kemal became a human dynamo; when things got boring, he tended to disappear into the bottle or the brothel. In 1913, Enver banished him to Sofia, the Bulgarian capital, making him military attaché to the Turkish embassy. There he gambled, drank, learned ballroom dancing and caught venereal disease - until the call came. In February 1915, he received orders to report to Turkish headquarters on the Gallipoli peninsula which was under attack from a British and Allied invasion fleet.

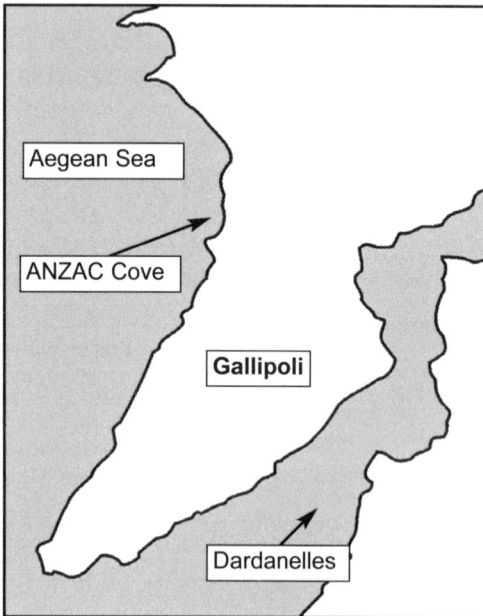

The British attacked Gallipoli because they wanted to open a second front against the Germans outside Western Europe and away from the horrors of trench warfare in

France and Belgium. They failed because of Mustafa Kemal. He inspired his men to quite incredible feats of courage and endurance and he himself seems to have had no concept of personal danger. He always walked slowly under enemy fire and once sat coolly smoking outside a trench while Australian artillery got their range on him. His men looked on with horrified fascination from below. At one point he was only saved from serious injury or even death when a piece of shrapnel was stopped by the watch in his breast pocket. Due to his leadership, in January 1916 the invaders were forced from the peninsula.

Defeat

Gallipoli, however successful for the Turks, was only an episode in the larger conflict and in 1918, when the First World War ended, nothing could disguise the fact that Turkey had picked the wrong side. It was shorn of all but its Anatolian heartland and a bit of Thrace.

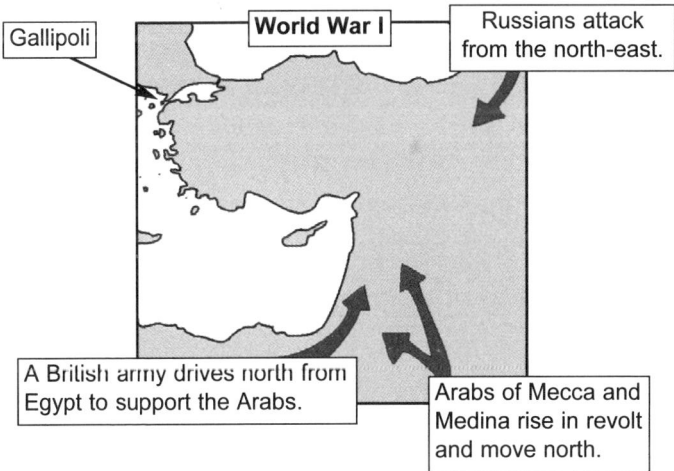

Gallipoli | **World War I** | Russians attack from the north-east.

A British army drives north from Egypt to support the Arabs.

Arabs of Mecca and Medina rise in revolt and move north.

That November (1918), British battleships steamed towards Constantinople. Soon the streets were full of British and Allied soldiers enjoying the sights. Enver and two other senior leaders of the Committee for Union and Progress fled forever in a German torpedo boat.

Unlike Turkey, Greece had been on the winning side during the war. Now it cashed in its chips. Smyrna (Izmir), the second largest city in Turkey, had a large Greek population. With British and Allied approval, the Greek army took it over on 15 May 1919 and the local Greeks immediately massacred all the Turks that they could lay their hands on. The Turkish government could do nothing because the Turkish head of state was none other than feeble Sultan Mehmet V, Abdul Hamid's replacement, and Sultan Mehmet was prepared to agree to practically anything in return for a quiet life.

Meanwhile, in the rest of Anatolia, ordinary Turks seethed with resentment. It only needed a spark to set off further fighting. Having no other capable general to turn to, Sultan Mehmet asked Mustafa Kemal to keep order in the eastern provinces.

He couldn't have made a worse choice. Mustafa Kemal felt humiliated by the British and Allied presence in Constantinople and by the atrocities in Smyrna. He was already plotting how to resist British influence. If ever there was a spark, he was it. He seized his chance before the sultan could change his mind, flung some clothes in a suitcase and boarded a battered steamer bound for Samsun on the Black Sea. From there he travelled inland. Once in Central Anatolia and out from under British eyes, he set about building a centre of resistance to all foreign interference in his country.

Ankara

Ankara, Angora as it used to be called, was once most famous for a certain type of soft wool produced by plucking rather than shearing. It was a run-down, out-of-the-way sort of place but that made it attractive to Mustafa Kemal. Here he set up (April 1920) an alternative government, the 'Grand National Assembly', away from occupied Constantinople. Ankara, in the landlocked heart of Anatolia, was a long way away from British pressure.

1920s Ankara was nothing much to look at for a fledgling capital city. It had been badly damaged by a fire during the war and the dirt streets were lined with charred buildings. There was so little accommodation that delegates to the new government were reduced to sleeping in hallways and cupboards before they could get properly settled. It was all very *ad hoc*. The sultan's stooge government in Constantinople had declared Mustafa Kemal an infidel to be shot on sight. He and his closest companion, Mehmet Arif, slept with their clothes on and with horses ready harnessed in case they had to make a sudden run for it.

If you're in Ankara
The Republic Museum on Cumhuriyet Bulvari was the second home of the Turkish Grand National Assembly (1924-61). It was in this building that Kemal Ataturk drove through all of his major reforms. The main assembly hall contains waxwork models and depicts a speech given by Ataturk in October 1927.

The last struggle

Meanwhile the Greeks kept in with the British and their allies. Their charming and plausible Prime Minister, Eleftherios Venizelos, offered his assistance in re-establishing 'law and order' in Anatolia. He dreamed of extending Greek rule to include all the Mediterranean coast, the coastal strip where the cities of the Ancient Greeks had flourished so many centuries before. The British found his offer attractive because they themselves were running down their armed services now that the war was over.

Not so the Greeks, who had been buying up surplus war stock and were ready for a fight. Sure enough, in January 1921 they cut through the disorganised Turkish forces and fought their way deep into Anatolia, terrorising the local population as they moved forward. The Turks were in danger of being completely overwhelmed. From his base in Ankara, Mustafa Kemal called on the entire Turkish population to support the war effort. Every household under the control of his forces had to supply underwear, socks and shoes for the fighting men. Women carried supplies and even heavy shells to the men at the forward positions.

Such dedication by itself would not have been enough against superior Greek armaments but for one factor: the Turks had Mustafa Kemal and the Greeks didn't. Mustafa Kemal was a military genius. He withdrew his forces before the Greek advance thus deliberately stretching their supply lines. In August 1921, the Greeks were decisively defeated at the Battle of Sakkaria, halfway between Eskisehir and Ankara. In the final days of the battle Greek supplies were so low that they'd even run out of water.

In brief - the post-war years	
1920	Greeks invade deep into Anatolia. Massacres of Turkish civilians.
July 1921	Greeks reach as far as the railway junction of Eskisehir.
August 1921	Decisive Battle of Sakkaria. Greek supply lines are too long. Greeks forced to retreat.
1922	Turkish counter attack. Greeks are forced back on Smyrna. Massacres of Greek civilians.

A blot on the landscape

What followed was one of the worst things Mustafa Kemal ever did, or rather, allowed to happen. After the Battle of Sakkaria the Turks forced the Greeks back towards the coast and towards Smyrna, terrorising the local Greek population in their turn. In September 1922 they retook Smyrna in a brutal orgy of massacre and rape. True, Mustafa Kemal threatened to execute Turkish soldiers who hurt civilians but he did nothing to enforce his threat. A fire destroyed all but the old Turkish quarter of the city.

When the killing stopped and the fire died down, there was very little left of Greek Smyrna or its inhabitants.

There was one final problem. A Greek army was still stationed on Turkish soil over the water in Thrace - and the British controlled a 'neutral zone' around the Dardanelles and the Turks couldn't cross the Dardanelles without breaking through it. Mustafa Kemal marched north. There was a stand-off between the British and Turkish armies with a mere twenty metres between them. A battle seemed almost inevitable and the British were backed up by their fleet with all its enormous guns.

Once again Mustafa Kemal showed his genius. He ordered his men to advance right up to the British lines - but with their rifles pointing down.

It was the British who blinked first. After lengthy negotiations they promised to order the Greeks out of Thrace - if the Turks would just back off a bit. A treaty was signed and the British and their Allies agreed to leave Turkish soil.

Turkey was saved.

Population Exchange

One of the saddest events in the history of modern Greece and Turkey took place following an agreement between the Turkish and Greek governments in 1923, at the end of the Greek-Turkish War. Around 1,300,000 Greeks were expelled from Turkey to Greece and around 400,000 Turks were expelled from Greece to Turkey.

ALL CHANGE
ENTER THE HERO

In brief - the reforms

November 1922	Sultanate abolished.
October 1923	Ankara becomes the official capital of Turkey and Turkey is declared a republic.
March 1924	Caliphate abolished.
April 1925	Wearing of the fez made illegal. All must wear modern, western headware.
November 1928	Arabic alphabet replaced by western alphabet.
1930	Name of Constantinople changed to Istanbul.
1934	Turks take surnames. Mustafa Kemal named Ataturk (Father of the Turks)
1934	Women get the vote.

Out with the old

On 17 November 1922, Mehmet VI, the brother of Mehmet V and the very last of the Ottoman sultans, clambered into a British ambulance at the Palace of Yildiz and was driven through autumn drizzle to a quayside along from the Golden Horn. From there he was taken out to the British battleship *Malaya* anchored in the Bosphorus and then he steamed off to exile in Italy. With him went his small son, a eunuch and a bag of gold coffee-cups. He was joined later by his five wives. Thus ended the Ottoman Empire.

Turkey was becoming a republic. This was officially

declared the following year, 29 October 1923. The capital was moved to Ankara and Mustafa Kemal became the first President. Surely no one has ever had such an effect on their country in such a short space of time.

Headgear

Mustafa Kemal regarded organised religion as a curse. His first move was to abolish the Caliphate, the office of leader of the Muslim world. The positions of Caliph and Sultan had once been held jointly by the reigning sultan but by 1924 they were separated. The Caliph, Abdul Mejid, was a brother of the former sultan but not the sultan himself. Annoyingly as far as Mustafa Kemal was concerned, although harmless, Abdul Mejid rather liked the trappings of office. He liked to travel in procession through the streets of Constantinople surrounded by a colourful retinue dressed in the full Ottoman gear. The sight of traditional clothing was extremely irritating to Mustafa Kemal. The Caliphate was abolished on 3 March 1924. A month later all religious courts were abolished.

Old-fashioned clothes, old-fashioned headgear in particular, meant old-fashioned social attitudes. The fez was outlawed in 1925 and for a while a lot of Turkish men were in an awkward situation because they didn't have anything else to put on their heads. There were tales of men working the fields in ostrich-plumed, female bonnets.

Shortly afterwards, the veil for women was also abolished, an incredible change for a conservative, Muslim country where female modesty had once been highly prized. It had been known for very modest women to wear their veils in the presence of male animals.

All change

And the changes kept coming. The poor Turks were shell shocked. They'd allowed an elemental demon to get his hands on their country and they seemed unable to resist. Imagine what would happen in the west if someone tried to change the weekend to Friday. There'd be riots. But that's what happened in Turkey, except the other way around. Mustafa Kemal also changed the calendar and modernised the way time was counted.

Even language was changed. Modern societies need family names as well as personal names. A telephone directory where the customers are split into a few large chunks under headings such as 'Rupert' and 'Sandra' or 'son of Rupert' or 'daughter of Sandra' wouldn't be much use. From 1934 all Turks had to take surnames. Mustafa Kemal himself became 'Mustafa Ataturk' meaning 'Mustafa, Father of the Turks'. Meanwhile Constantinople had become Istanbul, possibly from a Greek phrase meaning 'in the city', Smyrna had become Izmir, Adrianople had become Edirne and so on.

But the really major linguistic change came in 1928. Up to that time Turkish had always been written in the Arabic script, which is ideal for Arabic and very beautiful but less suited to Turkish. From November 1928, everyone had to write in the Roman alphabet with suitable, easy spellings and special accents to describe some sounds. The whole system was designed in about six weeks and Mustafa Kemal stumped round the country preaching the benefits. The new Turkish alphabet is more logical than its western brothers and it's a boon for visitors. Anyone can work out that *taksi* means 'taxi'.

Ataturk died on 10 November 1938, at 9.05 am in the morning according to the new system of time, of cirrhosis of the liver. He'd lived most of his adult life on a diet of coffee, alcohol and cigarettes, with food as an occasional interruption, so it should have been no great surprise, but somehow it was. Turkey was suddenly bereft of perhaps the most extraordinary figure it has ever produced out of a great gallery of extraordinary figures.

It is thanks to Ataturk more than any other individual that Turkey has taken its place in the modern world.

Getting up-to-date
The elemental demon had died. He left behind him a country half modernised and half traditional. 1930s Istanbul was a creaking compromise where the foghorns of the ships blended with the wail of the muezzin, and where some women washed their clothes at the water's edge while others took jobs in offices and factories. Out in the countryside things were even more traditional. There were still more horses than tractors, in fact there weren't many tractors worth speaking of for years to come.

The change from hidebound Ottoman Empire to dynamic modern state was bound to be difficult. Ataturk had been too strong willed and dictatorial for a true democrat. He left behind him a very rigid system and it was years after his death before proper, multi-party democracy had a chance. That was in the 1950s when a new party, the Democratic Party, took power. Unfortunately, this new party soon turned ugly. Journalists were fined and printing presses were closed down, as were some of the smaller opposition parties. At the same time, to appease more conservative elements in society, religious instruction was allowed back into schools and the call to prayer at the mosque could be sung in Arabic once more.

Army manoeuvres

Armies are often the bad guys when it comes to politics, but the Turkish army is a bit different. It sees itself as the guardian of Ataturk's inheritance. Since his death, it has taken power three times, each time in order to preserve his legacy, and each time it has returned to barracks of its own accord.

By 1960, the Democratic Party leadership had begun to threaten many of Ataturk's reforms, and it looked like they intended to ban all effective opposition, which would have been tantamount to setting up a dictatorship. To head off this possibility, the army stepped in for the first time. Having seized the reins of government, the generals abolished the Democratic Party and executed its Prime Minister for corruption along with two other ministers. Next year, with almost miraculous self-restraint and having organised a general election, the generals retired to barracks to see how the new lot of politicians would get on.

The second time the army intervened was in 1970. By that time, extremist parties of both left and right, in particular the 'Grey Wolves', a ruthless, right-wing, paramilitary organisation, were causing fear and mayhem among the general population. There was also fear of armed rebellion among the minority Kurds in the east. The army established martial law in several provinces then returned to barracks three years later.

The third and, hopefully, the last time that the army took over was in 1980 and this time the gloves were off. Political parties were dissolved and there were mass arrests of extremists and supposed extremists. Yet once again the soldiers returned to barracks. And that's where they've stayed ever since.

POSTSCRIPT

Thousands of years have passed since the people of Çatal Höyük buried their dead beneath the bed and painted that extraordinary map on the wall. One might have expected, after so many centuries of civilisation, that things would start to settle down a bit. But no, Turkey is remarkably young and energetic for somewhere so old.

East of the Golden Horn, on the European side of Istanbul, lies the district of Taksim, at its centre Taksim Square, the vibrant heart of the modern city. Head south-west from Taksim down the Istiklal Caddesi and you're in an up-market playground. Pedigree dogs, a most un-Islamic fashion statement, compete for space on the pavements with well-heeled crowds out to visit the clubs and restaurants. The girls and boys are dressed in the latest trends. The boutiques are as sophisticated as anything you'll see in Paris, London or Rome. You might as well be in a western capital city.

But travel to the outer suburbs and it's a different world. In recent years, large numbers of peasant families have migrated there from eastern and central Turkey and settled in cheap housing. They've brought their traditional culture with them. The men sip tea in the tea shops, the women wear headscarves, children play in the streets. You could be in Asia.

That's the glory of Turkey. It's more than a country. It's a complete world with more variety in it than some continents. It would repay a hundred visits if one only had the time. Nowhere else has its special, exuberant, unresolved mixture of east and west, of ancient and modern. And change is as much in the air as it was when Alexander the Great raced naked round the tomb of Achilles.

Which makes this short history into a description of work in progress.

Perhaps the best is still to come.

Cyprus

After Selim the Sot conquered Cyprus in 1570, it remained part of the Ottoman Empire for 344 years, producing delicious wine for his descendants. When the Greek mainland became independent in 1830, Cyprus remained part of the Ottoman Empire against the wishes of the Greek part of the island population. Finally, in 1914 at the start of World War I, it was annexed by Britain. Now at last, with the Christian British in charge, the Greeks expected *enosis*, their word for political union with the Greek mainland. It was not to be. A substantial Turkish minority on the island were very fearful of *enosis* and the British foresaw trouble if it went ahead.

Years went by. Impatient for change, some Greek Cypriots began a campaign of terror against opponents of enosis, both British and Greek. Turkish and Greek communities drew apart as a result and in the 1960s, fighting broke out. Then, on 15 June 1974, nationalist Greeks attacked the Presidential Palace and proclaimed an extreme advocate of *enosis* to be the new president. Back in Ankara, the Turkish government rushed to the support of the Cypriot Turks. A Turkish force was despatched and landed on the north of the island, driving the Greeks before them. Since that time, Cyprus has been divided into two parts, a southern Greek part and a northern, Turkish part. It's been a bone of contention between Greece and Turkey for years and for the time being the unhappy stalemate continues.

THE BYZANTINE EMPERORS

Constantinians
323-37 Constantine I, the Great
337-61 Constantius II
361-63 Julian the Apostate

Non-dynastic
363-4 Jovian

Valentinian-Theodosian
364-78 Valens
379-95 Theodoric I, the Great
395-408 Arcadius
408-50 Theodoric II
450-57 Marcian

Dynasty of Leo
457-74 Leo I
474 Leo II
474-91 Zeno
491-518 Anastasius I

Justinians
518-27 Justin I
527-65 Justinian I
565-78 Justin II
578-82 Tiberius II, Constantinus
582-602 Mauricius

Non-dynastic
602-10 Phocas I

Heraclian
610-41 Heraclius I
641 Constantine III
641 Heracleon
641-68 Constans II

668-85	Constantine IV
685-95	Justinian II, Slit-Nosed

Non-dynastic

695-98	Leontius II
698-705	Tiberius III, Apsimar

Heraclian

705-11	Justinian II (restored)

Non-dynastic

711-13	Philippicus
713-15	Anastasius II
715-17	Theodoric III

Isaurians

717-41	Leo III, the Isaurian
741-75	Constantine V
775-80	Leo IV
780-97	Constantine VI
797-802	Irene

Phocids

802-11	Nicephorus I
811	Stauracius
811-13	Michael I

Non-dynastic

813-20	Leo V, the Armenian

Phrygian

820-29	Michael II, the Stammerer
829-42	Theophilus I
842-67	Michael III, the Drunkard

Macedonian Emperors

867-86	Basil I, the Macedonian

886-912	Leo VI, the Wise
912-13	Alexander III
913-59	Constantine VII, Porphyrogenitos
919-44	Romanus I
959-63	Romanus II
963-69	Nicephorus II, Phocas
969-76	John I, Tzimisces
976-1025	Basil II, Bulgaroktonus
1025-8	Constantine VIII
1028-50	Zoë (Empress with co-rulers)
1028-34	Romanus III, Argyrus
1034-41	Michael IV, the Paphlagonian
1041-42	Michael V, Calaphates
1042-54	Constantine IX, Monomachus
1054-56	Theodora

Non-dynastic

1056-57	Michael VI, Stratioticus

Comnenids

1057-59	Isaac I, Comnenus

Doukid

1059-67	Constantine X, Dukas
1067	Andronicus
1067	Constantine XI
1067-71	Romanus IV, Diogenes
1071-78	Michael VII
1078-81	Nicephorus III

Comnenids (restored)

1081-1118	Alexius I, Comnenus
1118-43	John II
1143-80	Manuel I
1180-83	Alexius II
1183-85	Andronicus I

Angelid

1185-95	Isaac II
1195-1203	Alexius III
1203-04	Alexius IV
1204	Alexius V, the Bushy-Eyebrowed

Latin Emperors

1204-05	Baldwin I
1205-16	Henry VI
1216-17	Peter de Courtenay
1218-28	Robert de Courtenay
1228-61	Baldwin II

Nicaean Emperors

(They ruled in exile from Nicea.)

1204-22	Theodore I, Lascaris
1222-54	John Dukas Vatatzes
1254-59	Theodore II
1258-61	John IV, Doukas

Paleologi

1259-82	Michael VIII
1282-1328	Andronicus II
1328-41	Andronicus III
1341-47	John V
1347-54	John VI, Cantacuzene
1355-76	John V (restored)
1376-79	Andronicus IV
1379-91	John V (restored again)
1390	John VII (as co-Emperor)
1391-1425	Manuel II
1425-48	John VIII
1448-53	Constantine XI

SELJUK SULTANS OF ANATOLIA

1077-1086	Süleyman I
(interrregnum)	
1092-1107	Kiliç Arslan I
1107-1116	Melik Shah I
1116-1156	Masud I
1156-1192	Kiliç Arslan II
1192	Melik Shah II
1192-1196	Kay Khosru I
1196-1204	Süleyman II
1204-1205	Kiliç Arslan III
1205-1210	Kay Khosru I (second time)
1210-1220	Kay Kaus I
1220-1237	Kay Kobadh I
1237-1246	Kay Khosru II
1246-1257	Kay Kaus II
1248-1265	Kiliç Arslan IV
1249-1257	Kay Kobadh II
1265-1282	Kay Khosru III
1282-1284	Masud II
1284	Kay Kobadh III
1284-1293	Masud II (second time)
1293-1294 303-	Kay Kobadh III (second time)
1294-1301	Masud II (third time)
1301-1303	Kay Kobadh III (third time)
1303-1307	Masud II (fourth time)
1307	Masud III

OTTOMAN SULTANS

1300-26	Osman I, *Bey*
1326-60	Orkhan (first to take title of Sultan)
1360-89	Murad I, the Victorious
1389-1403	Bayezit I 'Yildirim' ('the Thunderbolt')
1403-1413	Interregnum
1413-21	Mehmet I
1421-45	Murad II
1451-81	Mehmet II 'the Conqueror'
1481-1512	Bayezit II
1512-1520	Selim I the Grim
1520-66	Suleiman I 'the Magnificent'
1566-74	Selim II, 'the Sot'
1574-95	Murad III
1595-1603	Mehmet III
1603-17	Ahmet I
1617-1618	Mustafa I
1618-22	Osman II
1623-40	Murad IV
1640-8	Ibrahim I
1648-87	Mehmet IV
1687-91	Suleiman II
1691-5	Ahmet II
1695-1703	Mustafa II
1703-30	Ahmet III
1730-54	Mahmud I
1754-7	Osman III
1757-74	Mustafa III
1774-89	Abdul Hamid I
1789-1807	Selim III

1807-8	Mustafa IV
1808-39	Mahmud II, the Reformer
1839-61	Abdul Mejid
1861-76	Abdul Aziz
1876	Murad IV
1876-1909	Abdul Hamid II
1909-18	Mehmet V, Reshat
1918-22	Mehmet VI, Vahideddin
1922-24	Abdul Mecit (Caliph only)

Important Dates

BCE

c.8500-7500	Çatal Höyük
c.1920-1780	Syrian merchants set up trading stations across southern Anatolia.
c.1750-1450	Hittite kingdoms
c.1450-1180	Hittite Empire
c.1343-1322	Reign of Hittite Emperor Suppiluliumas, and the high point of Hittite power
c.1250	Destruction of Troy IV, the Troy of Homer's Iliad.
c.1,000	Start of Greek migration to Aegean coast of Anatolia.
c.750	Midas founds the Phrygian Empire.
696	Gordium, capital of the Phrygians, destroyed.
667	Greek colony of Byzantium founded.
c640	Thales active in Miletus, start of the Golden Age of Greek philosophy.
337	Kingdom of Pontus founded in northern Anatolia.
334	Alexander the Great crosses the Dardanelles.
323	Alexander the Great dies at Babylon, start of the Hellenistic period. Anatolia ruled by Seleucis.
278	Gauls from central Europe invade Anatolia and settle in 'Galicia'.
130	Roman province of Asia Minor established with Pergamum as its capital.
81	Pontus comes under direct Roman rule.
67	Cilicia becomes a Roman province.

41	Antony meets Cleopatra in Tarsus.

AD

40-56	Journeys of St Paul of Tarsus, growth of the early Church.
323	Constantine becomes sole Roman Emperor.
324	Christianity becomes an official state religion of the Roman Empire.
330	Constantinople founded.
413	Walls of Theodoric begun.
537	Completion of Haghia Sophia
570	Birth of Mohammed
636	Heraclius defeated by the Arabs at the Battle of Yarmouk
669	First Arab attack on Constantinople
674	Invention of 'Greek Fire'
674-78	Second Arab attack on Constantinople
716-17	Third Arab attack on Constantinople
998	Formation of the Varangian Guard
1071	Romanus IV defeated by the Turks at the Battle of Manzikert.
1095-99	First Crusade
1204-61	Latin Emperors rule Constantinople after the Third Crusade.
1243	Seljuks defeated by the Mongols.
1320	Osman Bey takes Bithynia.
1321	Ottomans reach the Sea of Marmara.
1346	Ottoman troops cross into Europe for the first time.
1354	Ottomans take Gallipoli, their first permanent bridgehead in Europe.
1361	Edirne, capital of Thrace, captured by the Ottomans under Murad IV.

1365	Janissaries founded.
1371	Ottomans reach the Adriatic.
1389	First Battle of Kosovo, Ottomans defeat a Serb-led alliance.
1402	Bayezit captured and then driven to suicide by Tamerlane.
1448	Second Battle of Kosovo, Ottoman hold on Balkans consolidated.
1453	Mehmet the Conqueror takes Constantinople.
1454-81	Ottomans take Greece and the Crimea.
1517	Selim the Grim conquers Egypt and Syria.
1521	Suleiman the Magnificent takes Belgrade.
1523	Suleiman the Magnificent takes Rhodes.
1526	Battle of Mohacs, Hungary defeated.
1529	First siege of Vienna
1540s	Beginning of the Sultanate of Women
1566	Selim the Sot becomes sultan.
1570	Selim the Sot takes Cyprus.
1571	Battle of Lepanto, Ottoman fleet defeated by the Holy Alliance.
1595	On his accession to the throne Mehmet III has nineteen brothers and all his sisters strangled.
1603	Ahmet II introduces the 'Golden Cage' - end of tradition of fratricide.
1638	Abolition of the boy tribute
1648	Janissaries rebel and depose Mad Ibrahim.
1683	Second siege of Vienna

1699	Peace of Karlowitz, Ottomans lose Peleponnese, half of Hungary, Southern Ukraine and Azov.
1720s	First Ottoman ambassadors arrive in the west, also, second phase of tulip mania.
1776-	French officers employed to modernise the Ottoman army.
1779	Russia annexes the Crimea.
1808	Mahmud the Reformer becomes sultan.
1821	Start of the Greek Rebellion.
1827	Battle of Navarino, Ottoman fleet defeated.
1826	The Auspicious event (suppression of the Janissaries)
1829	Introduction of the fez, modernisation of the government
1830	Greek Independence
1853-56	Crimean War, Turkey the 'Sick Man of Europe'
1865	Society of New Ottomans formed.
1875	Ottoman Empire bankrupt
1876	New constitution declared, National Assembly with universal suffrage.
1878	National Assembly dissolved.
1878	Treaty of Berlin, Bulgaria becomes autonomous.
1894-95	First massacre of the Armenians
1906	Committee of Union and Progress (Young Turks) founded.
1909	Abdul Hamid deposed by Young Turks.
1914	Turkey joins World War I on the side of the Germans. Second massacre of the Armenians.
1915	Defence of Gallipoli

1919	Greeks land at Smyrna (Izmir).
1920	Ataturk founds Grand National Assembly in Ankara.
1921	Battle of Sakkaria, Greek invasion force defeated.
1922	Deposition of the last Ottoman sultan
1923	Turkey becomes a republic.

INDEX

Abdul Aziz, Sultan 83,84,85
Abdul Hamid I, Sultan 74
Abdul Hamid II, Sultan 82,
  83,85,86,87,89,90,91,92,
  93,96
Abdul Mejid, Caliph 102
Abdul Mejid, Sultan 79,80,
  82,83,
Achilles 20,108
Adana 22
Adrianople see Edirne
Agri Dağ 13,14
Ahmed III, Sultan 73
Ahmet II, Sultan 63
Albanians 67
Alemdar Mustafa 75,76
Alexander the Great 7,12,
  19-23,24,30,108
Alexandria 24
Alp Arslan 41
Anatolia 13,14,17,20,27,28,
  34,42,43,68,73,88,95
Anaximander 21
Ankara 12, 97,98,99,101,
  102
Ankara, Battle of 40,45
Anthemius of Tralles 34
Antioch 24
Antipater 23
Arabs, 9,36,95
Ararat, Mount see Agri
  Dağ
Armenians 47,67,89,93-100

Artemis see Diana of the
  Ephesians
Arzawan 17,18
Asia (the Roman province)
  27
Asia Minor 11,13
Ataturk, Kemal 82,93-100,
  102-104,105
Athene 30
Auspicious Event 66,77
Avars 9

Babylon 23
Baghdad 41
Baghdad Railway 22
Balkans 11,43,44,48,60,85,
  93
Barbarossa 61
Barton, Edward 65
Basil II, Emperor 38
Basil II, Emperor 38
Bektashi dervishes 55
Belgrade 54,58
Belisarius 32,33
Berlin, Treaty of 88
Besma 79,80
Beyazit I, Sultan 40,44,45,
  47,56
Beyazit II, Sultan 48
Beylerbi Palace 83
Bithynia 27,40,42
black eunuchs 64,76
Black Sea 13,14

Blackbird Field, Battle of 40,44
Blue Mosque 78
Bodrum *see* Halicarnassus
Bogazkale 17
Bosphorus 8,51,60,80,82, 83,85,86,87,101
Bulgaria 85,88
Bulgarians 84,93
Bulgars 9
Bursa 42
Byron, George Gordon, Lord, 80,81
Byzantine Empire 10,11,12, 29-39,42,46
Byzantium 20,29
Byzas 29

Calchedon 20
Caliphate 101,102
Callinicus 36
Cappadocia 27
Caspian Sea 41
Çatal Höyük 12,15-16,17, 107
Christ 27,28,30
Cilicia 26,27
Cilician Gates 22,26
Cleopatra, Queen 7,25,26, 27
Colophon 21
Columbus, Christopher 53
Committeee of Union and Progress 79,90,96
Constantine 'the Great', Emperor 19,27,29

Constantine XI 8,10,11
Constantinople 8,9,11,12, 19,27-8,29,30-1,36,37,39, 46,47,54,55,59-60,67,78, 101,103
Crimean War 79,81-82
Croesus, King 18
Crusaders 9,29,38-39,46
cuneiform 17
Cybele *see* Diana of the Ephesians
Cydnus, River 25,26
Cyprus 58,61,107

Dacia 27
Dardanelles 19,20,42,100
deaf mutes 49,65,66,76,87
Deli regiment 52
Democratic Party 104,105
devirshme 43,52,57,66
Diana of the Ephesians 23-24,25
Divan 56
Dolmabaçe Palace 80,82, 84
Dubucq de Rivery, Aimée 73-4,75,76

Edirne 11,42,88,93,103
Efes *see* Ephesus
Egypt 18,22,26,48,75,81,95
Elizabeth I, Queen 65
Enver Bey (Enver Pasha) 91,93,94,96
Ephesus 16,20,21,24,25,27

fez 101,102
fratricide 44,48,62-3
French Revolution 74

Galatia 27
Galicia 55
Gallipoli 94-5
Gate of Felicity 65
Golden Cage 58,63,64,66, 75
Golden Gate 6
Golden Horn 8,10,65,80, 101,107
Golden Road 74,76
Gordium 18,22,23
Gordius, King 22
Grand Mufti 66
Grand National Assembly 91,97
Granicus, Battle of 22
Greece 23,43,81,96,100, 107
Greek Fire 36
Greek Independence 79,81
Greeks 6,8,9,20,24,47,67, 79,81,91,93,96,98
Grey Wolves 106

Haghia Sophia 10,11,31,32, 34,39,51,54,65,66,78
Halicarnassus 20,21
hamams 60
Harald Hardrada 38
Hastings, Battle of 38
Hellespont see Dardanelles
Heraclitus 21

Heraclius 21,29,34-35,37
Hippodrome 31,32,33,66, 77,78
Hittites 6,12,15,17-18
Holy Alliance 61
Homer 19,21
Hungary 54,58
Huns 31,39
Hypatius 32

Ibrahim I, Sultan 64,66
Ibrahim Pasha 81
Ibrahim, Vizier 50,57
Iconoclasm 29
Iliad 19
Iran see Persia
Isidore of Miletus 34
Istanbul (see also Constantinople) 102,103,104,107
ixarette 51
Izmir 21,96,99-100,103

Janissaries 40,43,52,55,63, 66-7,71,72,75,76-7,79
Jerusalem 35,36,37,38
Jews 27,67
John of Austria 61,62
Josephine Bonaparte, Empress 74,75
Julian the Apostate 29
Justinian Rhinometus, Emperor 36
Justinian, Emperor 28,29, 32-34

Kara Djehennem 77
Kara Mustafa, Vizier 71
Karlowitz, Peace of 71
Knights of Saint John 54
Konya 15,16
Kosovo Polje *see* Blackbird Field
Kubaba *see* Diana of the Ephesians
Küçüksu Kasri Palace 82
Kul 57
Kurds 106

Lazar, Prince and Saint 44
Lepanto, Battle of 58,61-62
Lycia 18,27
Lycus, River 11
Lydians 15,18

Maeander, River 21
Mahmud II 'the Reformer', Sultan 66,75,76,77,79
Malazgirt 37
Manzikert, Battle of 36,37, 38,40,42
Mark Antony 19,24-25,26, 27
Marmara, Sea of 5,8,42,51, 64
Mehmet Arif 97
Mehmet I, Sultan 43,45
Mehmet II 'the Conqueror', Sultan 8,9,10,11,31,46, 47,48
Mehmet III, Sultan 63
Mehmet IV, Sultan 71

Mehmet V, Sultan 87,92,96
Mehmet VI, Sultan 101
Mehmet Pasha 81
Mellart, James 15,16
Mesalongi 80
Midas, King 18,23
Midhat Pasha 84,85,86
Miletus 20,21
millets 47
Milosh Obravitch 44
Mohacs, Battle of 54
Mohammed, Prophet 35,37, 77
Mongols 42
Moniteur de l'Orient 74
Montague, Lady Mary Wortley 60
Montenegrins 93
Montenegro 88
Murad I, Sultan 42,43,44
Murad II, Sultan 45
Murad III, Sultan 63
Murad IV, Sultan 66,85
Murad V, Sultan 87
Mustafa Kemal *see* Ataturk, Kemal
Mustafa IV, Sultan 75,76

Napoleon Bonaparte 74,75
Napoleonic Wars 75
National Assembly 79,85, 86,91,92
Navarino, Battle of 79,81
New Army 74,75,77
Nicaea 42
Nightingale, Florence 82

Noah 30

Orient Express 89
Orkhan 42,44
Osman I, Sultan 12,40,42, 43,44
Osman II, Sultan 49

Palestine 22,27,48
Parsees 16
Pergamum 20,24
Persia 11,20,48
Persians 9,18,19,22,23,34, 35
Phillip II, King 61
Phocas, Emperor 35
Phrygians 6,15,18,22,23,24
Plevna, Battle of 88
Plutarch 25
Pontic Mountains 13,14
Pontus 27
population exchange 91, 100
Ptolemy 23

Rhodes 54
Romania 88
Romans 12,19,24-9
Romanus IV, Emperor 36, 37,38,42
Roxelana 50,55-57,58,59
Russ 9
Russians 73,79,82,88,95
Rustem Pasha, Vizier 55
Saint Gotthard, Battle of 72

Saint Paul 19,27
Sakkaria, Battle of 91,98-99
Salonika 90,91
Scutari 82
Seleucis 23
Selim 'the Grim', Sultan 48
Selim 'the Sot', Sultan 41, 59,60,61,62,63,107
Selim III, Sultan 74,75,76
Seljuk Empire 12,41-42
Serbia 88
Serbs 93
Shakespeare, William 25
Sinan the Architect 54-55, 63
slaves 42,43,54,57,62,64, 67-8,80
Smyrna see Izmir
Society of New Ottomans 79,83,84,90
Sofia 94
Sokollu Mehmet Pasha, Vizier 59,61
spahis 43,52
Sublime Porte 65
Suffi Islam 55
Suleiman 'the Magnificent' 7,12,50,53-61,73,80
Sultanate of Women 56
Syria 22,27,48

Tamerlane 40,45,56
Tarsus 19,22,25,26,27
Taurus Mountains 13,14,22
Thales 21